APPROACHES TO THE BACH CELLO SUITES

A HAND-BOOK FOR CELLISTS

by

BY   CHARLES MEDLAM

© Charles Medlam, 3rd Edition, 2023
ISBN 978-1-8382144-4-9

PREFACE

This little book emerged in response to questions asked by students and other teachers on various courses. Many of them are genuine questions from students, and some are questions devised by me, which I feel that cellists ought to be asking. Some are close to factual and therefore in some degree answerable. Some are more speculative but receive answers as devoid of conjecture as possible. Others are quite simply unanswerable but I have tried anyway. The cellist/artist/ human being is a pot which has been randomly filled with degrees of talent, life experience, emotional and processorial intelligence - and sheer information. It is this last aspect which my questions and answers attempt to address, and I hope that my unusual perspective as baroque cellist and bass violist with special interest in the French solo suite render me well-placed enough to dare to try. Like most musicians I have always wondered where the miracle which is music comes from. Cellists in particular with their Bach suites, and musicians in general with most of their pieces have a habit of taking the material they are wrestling with for granted. They come, after all, from the teacher or the music shop much like other consumer items. But the thought should repeatedly sober us that the composer actually had to take out his pen and write notes on an empty piece of paper. My questions in part seek to wonder what influences and references Bach had in his head as he sharpened his quill and dipped it in the ink. It is heartening that the odd symbols he used to fill the empty lines are still part of our culture, and that we still feel the need to ponder and pick over them.

Since many of today's performers are as adept with libraries, sources and the mechanics of musicology as the musicologists themselves, I have not thought it useful to back up every quote with chapter and verse. (Source information can be found within the text itself.) This *parvum opus* is designed as a hand-book for cellists, whose interests will probably not be best served by copious notes hidden away at the end.

Thanks are due to Steven Isserlis, Alexander Baillie and Alberto Lysy, as well as to many less celebrated exponents, who have contributed questions and suggestions. Thanks are also due to the late Richard Campbell, who read through my efforts and helped to eliminate several grammatical clumsinesses and more than a few intellectual muddles; and to Terence Charlston for reading an early version and applying his forensic attention to detail, saving me from many a slip of the keyboard. Lawrence Dreyfus also lent his considerable experience and acumen, opening doors to new ways of thinking.

All the translations are my own and I am grateful to Ingrid, my German-speaking spouse of many years, for correcting and improving my efforts. I am on my own with the French, so must take full credit for any solecisms.

Female readers will hopefully forgive me the suppression of the clumsy formulation "his and hers" as in "clearly the front rank virtuoso can only play at his (or her) reliable best when playing the instrument he (or she) practises daily in its normal tuning" etc. And the ungainly "their" is no better. I have decided on the hopefully neutral and grammatically more tidy "his" to encompass the fairer sex as well, and must therefore accept any brickbats coming my way from that corner.

Thanks are due to the Staatsbibliothek in Berlin for permission to quote passages from Anna Magdalena and Kellner's manuscripts, to the Library of Congress for Du Buisson, and to the Jagiellonian Library in Krakow for Hotman.

CONTENTS

	page
PART I THE SUITE BEFORE BACH	4
PART I THE SUITE IN BACH'S TIME	12
PART 3 PERFORMING THE SUITES	20
PART 4 MISCELLANEOUS QUESTIONS	71

PART I   THE SUITE BEFORE BACH

****

At any given time thousands of people worldwide will be performing, practising, teaching or listening to Bach's Six Sonatas & Partitas for solo violin, or the Six Suites for unaccompanied violoncello. There cannot be many, or perhaps even any other set of works, which provoke such exhaustive study, discussion and enjoyment.

But even a genius of Bach's stature had to have models.

So how did the cello suites come about?
Some time in about 1715 Bach took the unprecedented step of sitting down in front of a blank sheet of paper to compose French suites for an instrument, which Anna Magdalena calls the violoncello.

How and when did the classical suite stabilise?
The idea of combining allemande, courante and sarabande occurred quite early on in the seventeenth century and was particularly popular in France and England. It is said that Louis XIII's sister, Henrietta Maria brought the sarabande to London when she married Charles I in 1625.
At that time a rhythmically complex courante or two was preceded by an exploratory allemande and rounded off with an elegant and probably quite sprightly sarabande. By mid-century the sarabande had steadied and began to feel more like a slow movement. During the 1650s, as if by some formal agreement, Froberger for the keyboard in Vienna, Gaultier for the lute in Paris, and Playford in London began to add a gigue. Composers then started to add a prelude (often without barlines) and insert "*galanteries*" between the sarabande and the gigue. By about the time of Bach's birth therefore, the French suite was a fully mature vehicle.

Bach's cello suites are all French dance suites in the classical mould with the conventional allemande, courante, sarabande and gigue preceded by a prelude and with a minuet, bourrée or gavotte before the final gigue.

How did he arrive at the *Frenchness* of the suites?
If there were no actual antecedents for cello suites, Bach would certainly have been very familiar with the idiom, and would have known any number of French harpsichord suites by German and French composers. Gerber writes in his *Historisch-Biographisches Lexicon der Tonkünstler* of 1790:

"Couperins Klaviersachen, die der große Seb.Bach besonders schätzte und seinen Schülern empfahl, sind noch in unsern Zeiten der Vergessenheit entzogen worden"

Couperin's keyboard pieces, which the great Sebastian Bach especially prized and recommended to his pupils, have in our times been rescued from obscurity.

Georg Muffat's two *Florilegiums*, suites of five-part French style orchestral music, were published in Augsburg in 1695 and Passau in 1698. Other small German courts were busy cultivating the French style and building chateaus in imitation of Versailles. As early as 1663 in Leipzig and Erfurt Johann Caspar Horn published two collections of :

Grossen Balletten, welche allhier vor wenig Jahren nicht sonder Gratie fürgestellet worden, nach der lustigen Französischen Manier zu spielen.

Dances, to be played in the light, airy French manner, presented with some acclaim a few years ago.

Are there any other French suites for solo bass instrument?
The English language has, surprisingly, adopted the term *viola da gamba* (often abbreviated to just *gamba*) to describe the bass instrument of the viol family. I prefer the unpretentious" bass viol" (as in treble and tenor viol) and will henceforth refer to the instrument as such.

The two families of string instruments, viols and violins, were clearly defined by about 1550. Until about 1650, the (loud) violins played dance and church music, and the (quiet) viols played sophisticated fantasies and consorts in the chamber. Thereafter the violin was fully accepted as an instrument for domestic music-making and ousted all viols but the bass, which became the string instrument of choice for aristocrat, professional and bourgeois. Numerous members of the French and English royal families added proficiency on it to their other accomplishments, and literally hundreds of dance movements for solo bass viol composed between 1650 and 1700 survive in manuscripts.

The main figures in this repertoire are **Nicolas Hotman, Le Sieur Dubuisson, Le Sieur de Machy and Jean de Sainte-Colomb**e.

In his *Traité de Viole* of 1687 Jean Rousseau describes Nicolas Hotman's playing and the status of the viol:

La tendresse de son Jeu venoit de ces beaux coups d'archet qu'il animoit, & qu'il adoucissoit avec tant d'adresse & si à propos, qu'il charmoit tous ceux qui l'entendoient, & c'est ce qui a commencé à donner la perfection à la viole, & à la faire estimer preferablement à tous les autres Instruments.

The tenderness of Hotman's playing came from those beautiful bow strokes which he animated or softened with such skill and so appropriately, that he charmed all those who heard him. And it was this which started to bring the viol to perfection, and which caused it to be admired more than any other instrument.

Engraving by Van Merle after S. Bénard

Nicolas Hotman, born in Brussels around 1615 was, like many at that time, both lutanist and violist. He was part of the Duc d'Orléans' music establishment from 1655 and subsequently at court. He died in 1663 and his are the first surviving suites for bass instrument with the classical core of allemande, courante, sarabande, gigue. He taught both de Machy and Sainte-Colombe.

Dubuisson (? - 1688) left well over a hundred compositions for unaccompanied bass viol, which are found in six manuscripts of French, English, Dutch, and German provenance in libraries throughout Europe and the United States. The earliest is from 1666 (Washington, DC., Library of Congress) and contains four suites in staff notation and two pieces in tablature. Each of these suites comprise the sequence prelude-allemande-courante-sarabande-gigue, the earliest French source consistently to add a prelude.

Prelude by Dubuisson dated *Le premier Jour de Septembre* (the first day of September) *1666* from Library of Congress Ms M2.1.T2.17C p.2 with the tuning of the six-string bass viol at the foot of the first page.

Le Sieur de Machy was the first to publish suites for solo bass viol. His *Pièces de Violle* of 1685 consists of four suites in staff notation and four in tablature. Seven of the suites start with the normal prelude/allemande/courante/sarabande/gigue, and finish with a gavotte and menuet, but the fourth suite in staff notation ends with a gavotte en rondeau and chaconne.

Prelude non-mesurée from DeMachy's *Pièces de Violle* 1685 p.44

Perhaps because he was a Protestant and had to maintain a low profile after the repeal of the Edict of Nantes in 1685 (which had guaranteed freedom of confession), we know very little about **Jean de Sainte-Colombe** - not even his dates. He is credited with the addition of the seventh string (a low AA) on the bass viol, taught Marin Marais, and gave concerts with his daughters. He left sixty-seven *Concerts à Deux Violes Esgales*, (pieces for two equal viols) and some hundred and forty solo pieces grouped usually by key. These can be assembled into suites but the intention is far from clear.

Sarabande by Sainte-Colombe from p.21 of Manuscript M.3 from the Bibliothèque Municipale de Tournus

Marin Marais (1656-1728) is the undisputed classicist of the bass viol in France. He learnt with Sainte-Colombe and studied composition with Lully, in whose operas he performed as continuo player. His five books of pieces (1686, 1701, 1711, 1717 and 1725) are the staple diet of any bass violist attempting to come to terms with the forms, techniques and spirit of the French bass viol repertoire. In the first two books the classical suite predominates. Subsequently more and more "*pièces*" appear with programmatic content and eccentric titles, reflecting a shift in taste from the classical to the rococo. This coincides more or less exactly with the death of Louis XIV in 1715. A few manuscript solo suites survive, which are similar and in some cases identical to the pieces in his first book. These clearly show the transition from the normal unaccompanied suite of the seventeenth century, to the normal accompanied (i.e. with a basso continuo of harpsichord and second bass viol) of the eighteenth.

Medallion of Marin Marais from Titon du Tillet's *Le Parnasse François* 1732 p.32

Marais was certainly known in Germany. His entry in Johann Gottfried Walther's Musikalisches Lexicon, Leipzig 1732, reads:

ein unvergleichlicher französischer Gambist, dessen Werke in ganz Europa bekannt sind.

an incomparable French violist, whose works are known all over Europe.

What was the motive for French composers to write all these suites for solo bass viol?
The viol played a central a role in domestic music-making, comparable to that of the piano in the nineteenth and into the twentieth century. You could play it alone or with others, sing to it and even transcribe popular songs or dances for it.

Dance suites could be:
a) performance material for the virtuoso, whose instrument is superlatively transportable to any part of his patron's *chateau* or *palais,*
b) teaching material for the *maîtres de viole*, with the *doubles* perhaps representing challenges for the more advanced pupils,
c) rehearsal music to practise the steps for social dancing, with frequent repetitions beneficial to both player and dancer, giving rise to experiments with variations and ornamentation.

What other works for bass viol could have fed Bach's imagination?
In addition to the many unpublished and possibly amateurish works for solo bass viol in his own circle, Bach would have probably been familiar with the work of the three most prominent German players of the previous generations, all of whom published collections of suites or sonatas.

Conrad Höffler (1647-1705) published a collection of classical suites with continuo in Nuremberg in 1695.

Some of **Auguste Kühnel (1645-1699)**'s suites of 1698 can be played as solos, as he reminds us in the preface.

Hierbey habe ich auch noch erinneren wollen, daß ich die ersten drey Sonaten à 2 und die letzten vier Suiten solo, so gesetzt habe, daß sie auch ohne Basso Continuo können gespielt werden.

And I also wanted here to remind the performer, that I have set the first three sonatas and the last four suites, so that they can be played without basso continuo.

And **Johann Schenck (1660-1712)**'s Sonate VI from Echo du Danube Op. IX printed in Amsterdam around 1700 is a genuine solo sonata with abstract movements, "improvised" sections, and fugues. Schenck's work contains particularly fine examples of how to write contrapuntally for the bass viol in a manner quite similar to Bach's violin fugues.

from the title page of Schenck's *L'Echo Du Danube Op.IX* c.1700

Four anonymous suites can be found in a manuscript dating from around 1680 in the Moravian Museum in Brno, Czechia, (MS D 189). All contain the four major movements, but not necessarily in the classical order. Three have a praeambulum and finale, and suites 2 and 3 have gavottes in the "wrong" place. About half the movements have ornamented repeats called *variatio* in the style of the French "*maîtres de viole*", whose influence is much in evidence. It is impossible to estimate how many such manuscripts were in circulation in the German-speaking lands.

Did Bach know the music of the French *Maîtres de viole* ?
It is now worth examining in more detail the possible dissemination of French bass viol music into Saxony, in which the violist and diplomat Ernst Christian Hesse could well be a key figure.

Ernst Christian Hesse (1676-1762) was born in the Thuringian town of Grossengottern and spent his school years at Langensalza and Eisenach. It is possible that a youthful Bach, nine years his junior, might have met him or heard him play there. Ernst Christian was destined study law, but Landgraf Ernst Ludwig of Hesse-Darmstadt heard him play and immediately offered him an administrative post at court, presumably a sinecure. He was allowed to finish his law studies in Gießen, and on his return to court, was made war secretary, obtaining leave of absence between 1698 and 1701 to perfect his viol-playing in Paris. There, the story according to Marpurg goes, he studied with both Marin Marais and Antoine Forqueray, each of whom boasted of his talented pupil, until the ruse was discovered. In 1705 he journeyed to Hamburg, where he met Handel and Mattheson, in 1706 to Holland and England, settling in 1707 in Darmstadt, where he became *Kapelldirektor*. In 1708 we find him in Venice, where he met Vivaldi, subsequently moving to Rome, where he once again encountered Handel, who probably wrote the obbligato parts in *La Resurezzione* and *Tra le Fiamme* for him there. He played at court in Dresden in 1709 and in Vienna in 1710 before returning to Darmstadt. It is not fanciful to conjecture that apart from many pieces in manuscript he might have collected, the following publications might have found their way from France to Saxony in his luggage: Marin Marais Book I 1686 & Book II 1701; De Machy 1685; Jacques Morel 1709. And his purchases in Amsterdam might have included Schenck's *Tyd en Konst Oeffeningen Op.2* of 1688, the undated *Scherzi Musicale Op. 6*, *Le nymphe di Rheno Op.8*, and
L'Echo du Danube Op. 9, all of which appeared before 1706; as well as Carolus Hacquart's twelve French suites of 1701.

As a further example of such cosmopolitan intercourse we can mention the violist Johann Christian Hertel or Hextel (1699-1754), who studied with Hesse in Darmstadt. He was active at court in Eisenach from 1718, met Bach at Köthen in 1719 and visited him again in Leipzig in 1726. It is likely that he played the bass viol solos in the St. John (1724) and Matthew (1727) Passions. It is inconceivable that he would not have learnt the French style from Hesse.

Bach therefore met musicians who had had both direct and second-hand experience of the Parisian viol school and would have had many opportunities to inform himself about the latest developments in the city, which was the foremost forum for viol playing.

THE SUITE   A rough chronology
****

1630-1640
Allemande - Courante -Saraband

Hotman 1640-1660
Allemande - Courante -Sarabande - Gigue

Du Buisson 1660-1675
Prelude - Allemande - Courante -Sarabande - Gigue

De Machy 1675-85
Prelude - Allemande - Courante -Sarabande - Gigue - Gavotte - Menuet - (Chaconne)

Marin Marais 1686 (Book I)
Prelude - Allemande - Courante - Sarabande - Gigue - Gavotte - Menuet
or
Prelude - Allemande - Courante - Sarabande - Gigue - Gavotte en rondeau - Menuet - Gavotte - Fantaisie en echo - Chaconne

Bach c.1715
Prelude - Allemande - Courante -Sarabande - Menuet/Bourree/Gavotte - Gigue

PART 2 THE SUITE IN BACH'S TIME

****

Why did Bach write the suites ?
Bach did not write his suites for financial gain. The violoncello as solo instrument would have been close to unknown in Germany in the early 1700s and even in the large centres of population like London, Amsterdam and Venice, solos were a rarity at this time. The undated Paris edition of the famous Vivaldi sonatas did not emerge until 1740 at the earliest. In addition Bach served as court or church composer all his life, coming from a tradition in which free-lance work was discouraged or even contractually forbidden by the employer. In general the composer would only publish to enhance a patron's prestige, or in anticipation of a court or church appointment.

Nor, unlike the works for violin, did he write them in imitation of other similar works, for, with the exception of Domenico Gabrielli's *Ricercares* for solo cello written in Bologna in the 1680s for a five string cello probably tuned C G d g c, which he is unlikely to have known, there is, as far as we know, no precedent for solo cello music. Westhoff, Biber and others had written music for solo violin, but the cello was not yet quite ready for solo treatment. Bach's idea may have been to adapt this style for the more contrapuntally limited cello, leaving out multi-part fugues in favour of preludes and dances.

Possible motives for composing the suites:

1) As a young composer Bach would have wanted to get to grips with a new instrument, which was already present but only just beginning to be considered as a solo instrument in competition with the bass viol or as complement to the violin.

2) Various family members might have needed study material. It is not fanciful to see the suites, starting as they do with the easy keys of G, d and C and moving to more difficult Eb and c, as a book of progressively challenging studies. Indeed in the Paris edition of 1824 describes them as *Etudes.* By way of analogy the forty-eight keyboard preludes and fugues of the *Wohltemperiertes Klavier* (Well-tempered Clavier) were written or compiled for Bach's eldest son, the harpsichord and organ virtuoso Wilhelm Friedemann. Bach senior describes them on the title page as being:

"Zum Nutzen und Gebrauch der Lehr-begierigen Musicalischen Jugend, als auch derer in diesem studio schon habil seyenden besonderen Zeitvertreib auffgesetzet und verfertiget"

"Composed and compiled for the use and practice of young musicians, who are keen to learn as well as for those already well versed in the discipline"

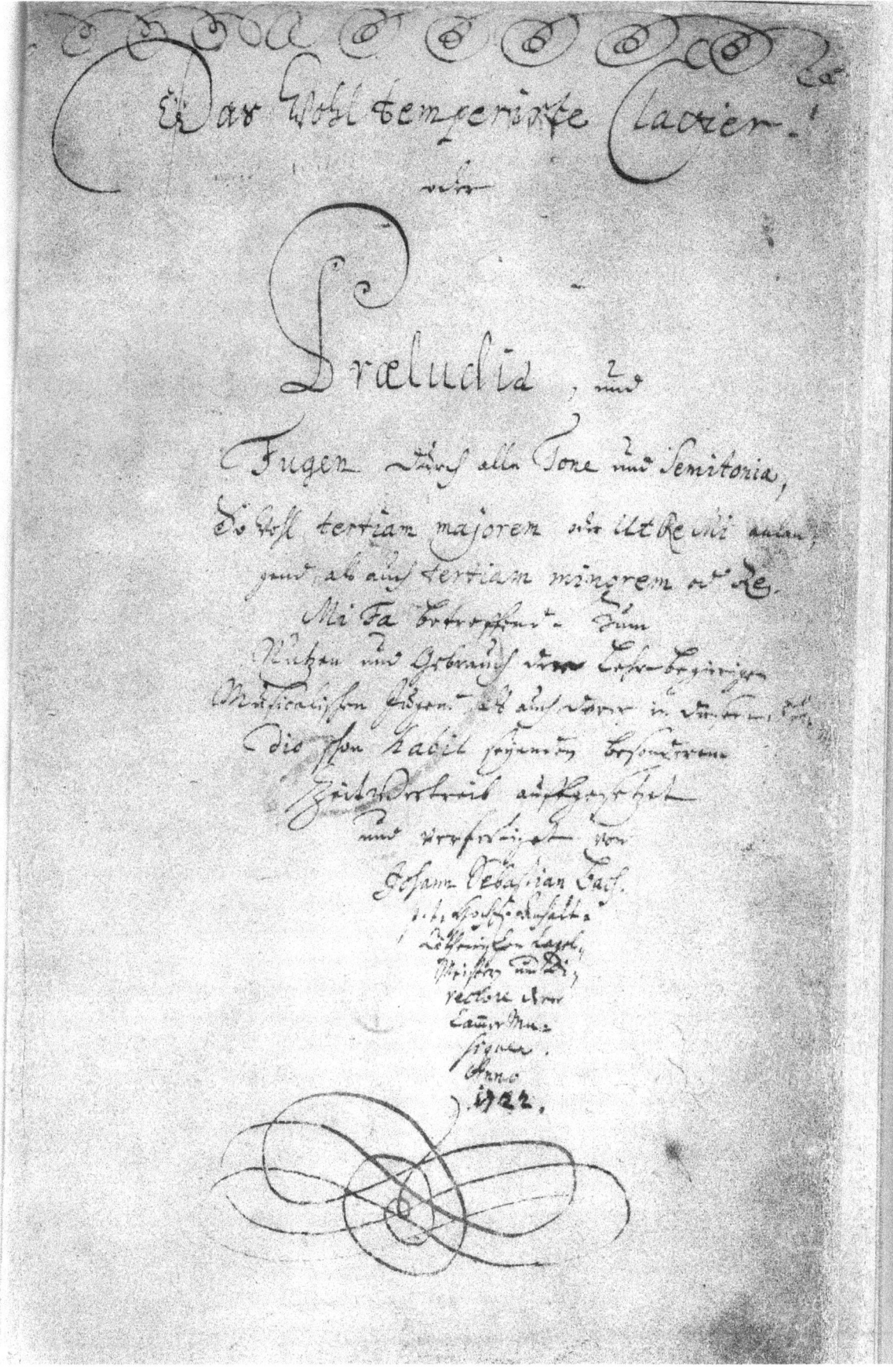

In a letter to Bach's first biographer, Johann Nikolaus Forkel (1749-1818), CPE Bach mentions the violin and cello works:

Er verstand die Möglichkeiten aller Geigeninstrumente vollkommen. Dies zeugen seine Soli für die Violine und für das Violoncell ohne Baß. Einer der größten Geiger sagte mir einmal, daß er nichts vollkommners, um ein guter Geiger zu werden, gesehen hätte u. nichts beßeres den Lehrbegierigen anrathen könnte, als obengennante Violinsoli ohne Baß.

He understood perfectly the possibilities of all the instruments of the violin family. The solos for violin and violoncello bear witness to this. One of the greatest violinists told me that, in order to become a good violinist, he had seen nothing better nor could recommend anything more fitting to the keen student, than the above mentioned violin solos without bass.

Letter to J.N Forkel in Göttingen, Hamburg late 1774 (III/801)

3) It is possible that a commission came from the court of Anhalt-Cöthen, where Bach worked from 1717-1723. Spitta (ii 4 and 100) cites the court violist Christian Ferdinand Abel (1683-1737) as possible candidate, but there is no evidence that he played the cello as well. Indeed at that time it was rare for a player to have played both instruments. Concert programmes from 1770s London show that Christian Ferdinand's son, Carl Friedrich, preferred to play his solos on the bass viol, but was prepared to play continuo on the cello in the same concert. Bach was a close friend of Christian Ferdinand Abel and godfather to his first daughter, and the association of the two families was to continue in the next generation in the form of the celebrated Bach/Abel concerts in London (1765-81), involving Johann Christian Bach and Carl Friedrich Abel. It is striking that Carl Friedrich's cello music, written some forty years later than the suites, is much less technically advanced.

Perhaps a more likely instigator or dedicatee is Christian Bernard Linigke (or Linike), the cellist of the Cöthen court orchestra. We cannot know whether the cellist commissioned the composer, or whether the composer needed a cellist to try out his new ideas.

In addition, we learn that Bach's employer at Cöthen, Prince Leopold, himself played the bass viol and perhaps even took one of the (diplomatically simple?) viol parts in the sixth Brandenburg Concerto.

4) Easily the strongest contender is the idea that Bach wrote the suites for himself to play on a *viola da spalla* (a large violin-family instrument played on the shoulder). We will examine this idea later in a discussion of the instrument intended for the suites.

In the same letter as above CPE Bach writes:
Als der größte Kenner u. Beurtheiler der Harmonie spielte er am liebsten die Bratsche mit angepaßter Stärcke u. Schwäche

As the greatest expert and judge of harmony he liked playing the viola best, with appropriate force or gentleness.

Nearly all virtuoso music up to the classical period was written by the performer himself. Bach surely wrote the suites the suites for himself to play on the nearest possible equivalent to his favourite instrument?

The problems with Anna Magdalena's manuscript
Aside from Anna Magdalena's manuscript, which is assumed to be a version of Johann Sebastian's fair copy, there are three roughly contemporary manuscripts before the first print of 1824.

1) Johann Peter Kellner (*Staatsbibliothek zu Berlin - Preußischer Kulturbesitz, Mus.ms.Bach P 804*) c.1726. The manuscript contains various other Bach pieces including the Sonatas and Partitas for solo violin. Kellner was a local organist who almost certainly knew Bach personally. It is not known whether he played the cello.

2) Anon (*Staatsbibliothek zu Berlin - Preußischer Kulturbesitz, Mus.ms.Bach P 289*) probably belonged at some stage to Johann Christoph Westphal, and was prepared by two different copyists. Westphal, in addition to his duties as an organist in Hamburg, had a business as printer and music dealer. He had works copied by hand for which the market was too small to merit the considerable costs of printing.

3) Anon (*Österreichische Nationalbibliothek Wien, Mus. Hs 5007*) had found its way into a Viennese sale-room by 1799 and is of mid- or north-German provenance.

There is also an arrangement for lute of the C minor suite written out by Johann Sebastian himself for a certain Monsieur Schouster sometime between 1727 and 1731.

The first printed edition of the whole set appeared in Paris and was published by Janet et Cotelle in about 1824. It was prepared by the cellist Louis Norblin (1781-1854), a professor at the Conservatoire, who called it *"Six Sonates ou Etudes pour le Violoncelle Solo composées par J.Sebastien Bach. Oeuvre Posthume"*. It looks very much as if he thought of the suites as just another set of useful *Etudes* for his pupils.

In contrast to Anna Magdalena's copy of Johann Sebastian's violin works, her version of the cello suites seems to have been written in some haste. We can assume that, with a weekly cantata to compose and parts to write out, a copious amount of music was prepared in the Bach household. Thus the slurs are sometimes quite distant from their intended notes, and she does not take the time (see the end of the C major gigue) to correct errors by scratching out wrong notes with a razor (the usual correction procedure of the time), but simply writes the names of the notes above them.

End of the C major Gigue from Anna Magdalena's manuscript

Some of the slurs are eminently sensible, practical and musical, others are hard to comprehend even if it were possible to identify exactly which notes they belonged to.

The contrast with the violin works, which have markedly fewer slurs, is striking.

Bach's fair copy of the Fugue from Sonata no.1 in G minor BWV 1001 with an almost total lack of slurs. *Staatsbibliothek Preußischer Kulturbestiz, Berlin, Mus.Ms. Bach P 967*

It is possible that Kellner's version was copied from Bach's own fair copy (now lost) and that it therefore represents a more reliable source. The slurs are more consistent and more carefully placed and, in contrast with that of Anna Magdalena, the whole manuscript looks as if it has been prepared with some care.

17

2nd Menuet from Suite No.2 in D minor in Kellner's careful copy.
Staatsbibliothek Preußischer Kulturbestiz, Berlin, Mus.Ms. Bach P 806

Can we make any judgements about the (presumed) inaccuracies of Anna Magdalena's script?

Below are three examples of the solo violin works with Bach's autograph fair copy on the left and Anna Magdalena's version on the right. Readers will draw their own conclusions from the differences, but one typical feature seems to be that Anna Magdalena's slurs (if they are copied at all) are habitually further to the right than in the original, a phenomenon known to all of us, who write out music in haste!

1) Presto from Sonata 1 for violin BWV 1001
2) Allegro from Sonata II for violin BWV 1003
3) Ciaccona from Partita II for violin BWV 1004

Which edition should I therefore use?
Given the source material available to an editor, it is not possible to make an edition, which is definitive in any sense of the word. The best solution for the player is to work from a clean modern edition (i.e. with the fewest editorial suggestions), refer continuously to Anna Magdalena and Kellner, and to try to arrive at the many difficult final performance decisions. Comparative editions with all the early versions are available for further study.

Why did Bach include so few "*galanteries*" in the suites?
In his own orchestral suites, Bach supplements the classical dances with a forlane, passepied, loure, polonaise and the famous badinerie. His *Clavir Ubung* (sic) published as Opus 1 in 1731 announces "andere Galanterien" (other *galant* pieces) next to the classical suite. These include such exotic titles as burlesca, scherzo and capriccio. Others at the time were including a musette, bransle, paysane or chaconne as well as lightly contrapuntal movements called fantaisie, boutade, or caprice. Bach could easily have drawn on these models to vary the form of the cello suites, but chose to leave the classical suite intact and only alternate the *galanteries* (between sarabande and gigue) in the form of pairs of menuets, bourrées and gavottes. Even the lute player and composer Silvius Leopold Weiss, the closest in time, place and approach, includes a paysanne and tombeau in his quite classical compilations. It is possible that Bach wanted to impose the rigour of classical suite form on himself as part of the compositional process, or was attracted by a symmetrical approach for the whole set. Equally, it might be that he simply did not see the possibility of adapting such dances to the constraints of the violoncello.

Are there other more direct influences?
The themes of the allemande and gigue in the C minor suite are similar enough to those in the F sharp minor *Pièces de Clavessin* of 1705 by Gaspard Le Roux (1660-1707) to merit mention. Bach uses the first bar and then makes no further reference to his models. Interestingly Le Roux's allemande is marked *allemande gaye,* and the gigue, called La Favouritte, is marked *un peu lentement.*

Gaspard Le Roux's *Pièces de Clavessin* 1705. Suite in f sharp minor p.52 and 55

The long pedal passage in the C major prelude is remarkably like the closing bars of the first allegro from Corelli's violin sonata Op.5/3 and may well derive from it.

Arcangelo Corelli Op. 5/3   final bars of Allegro

Alternatively, it might just reflect the organist's pleasure at improvising over a dominant pedal.

PART 3   PERFORMING THE SUITES

****

The technical detail of French bass viol music

It is worth returning to De Machy's 1685 suites, which furnish us with exceptional technical detail for the performer. In contrast to publications for the bass viol in Germany and the Netherlands, French and English composers were at pains to explain the many ornaments and other instructions in their publications. These were not just suggestions but represented the exact intentions of the composer, so much so that De Machy proposes in his preface that, if there be any performer who would like to confer with him on any aspect of his suites, he would be honoured to receive them on Saturdays between three and six o'clock and would show them "*la pratique de toutes les regles, dont j'ay parlé* (how to interpret all the rules which I have outlined)"! In his preface he lists eighteen ornaments, which he calls *agrémens*. There are trills and mordents of various sorts, two sorts of vibrato, the slur (i.e. playing two or more notes under the same bow) and perhaps most interestingly for the cellist, the *tenüe*. This indicates that, where possible, a finger must be left down to enhance the harmonic framework.

This technique had been in common use for some time, as Christopher Simpson explains on page 5 of Part I of his treatise on viol playing, the *Division-Viol* of 1665:

When you set any finger down, hold it on there; and play the following Notes with other fingers, until some occasion require the taking off. This is done to continue the Sound of a Note when the Bow hath left it.

In another context De Machy explains that

" *je n'explique cela que pour prouver la necessité qu'il y a de faire harmonie quand on jouë seul, puisque l'on convient qu'elle est l'âme de la Musique*"

I explain this only to emphasise how necessary it is to make harmony when one plays unaccompanied, since it is agreed that this is the soul of Music.

This is superlatively useful advice for the cellist.

In De Machy's publication there are four suites in staff notation and four in tablature. The music in staff notation is printed with bowing and fingering instructions for every note. This is not necessary for the other suites, since tablature is itself a fingering. Tablature assumes that everything is played in the first position using open strings. This precise notation provides a very reliable route to the technical mind-set of the composer, as well as pointing out several features of grammar. Vibrato is listed with the ornaments and notated when desired. The fourth finger vibrato was executed with the same rocking motion of the wrist which every cellist uses today. For the other fingers, the "*flattement*" was chosen, whereby the next finger up was placed close to the desired note and either rocked with the wrist as above, or trilled using just the finger itself. This ornament is one of the most characteristic features of bass viol technique, and though it works best on fretted instruments, may have transferred to the cello.

from De Machy's *Pièces de Violle* 1685. Table of ornaments P.13

Marin Marais's first book of bass viol pieces published in 1686 has a similar but less exhaustive table of *agrémens*. He lists two different trills, the *tenüe*, vibrato and the rare *coulé du doigt* (slide), which indicates a semi-tone *portamento* used only in programmatic pieces. (See his *Tombeau pour Mr. de Ste Colombe* below).

Thus we can say that Bach or any other German composer or player, assuming he knew this music or music similar to it, had a complete technical and grammatical structure on which to base the composition of suites for bass instruments.

De Machy's music and its notation is as useful to us today as to a foreign composer or player then. Our distance from it is merely that of time, not place.

What is tablature?
Since many of the early seventeenth viol players were also lutanists, it was natural that they would have written out their viol pieces in tablature. Tablature is a system of notation used by players of plucked instruments from about the early 16th century onwards, and still in use by guitarists today. Rather than notes on the lines of staff notation, the player is shown which finger to use on which string. The rhythm is indicated above by little half, quarter, sixteenth notes etc. This method is particularly practical if the lute, guitar, or viol uses several different tunings. Close to sixty different tunings for the lyra viol (a style of playing on the bass viol which was very popular in England between about 1610 and 1660) are recorded.

To all intents and purposes Biber notates his *scordatura* violin sonatas in tablature, but using staff notation. He uses fourteen different tunings in his Rosary Sonatas. Here the violinist plays as if his instrument were tuned normally using the fingers which he would normally use, but the differently tuned strings produce a different result. This may be one of the models for Bach in the notation of the fifth suite.

It is no accident that the use of tablature dies out at the same time as the experiments with different tunings. By about 1700 the use of multiple tunings for any one instrument is rare.

Sarabande from DeMachy's *Pièces de Violle* 1685 p.20 demonstrating that violists were still using tablature until the last years of the seventeenth century

Should I use vibrato: was it used at that time? were there any rules about when to use it?
Vibrato, if mentioned at all, is included in the list of ornaments in seventeenth and eighteenth century treatises and prefaces. From a technical standpoint, the chordal mind set of Bach's player (i.e. leaving fingers down to make harmony) would preclude the more or less permanent vibrato of the modern virtuoso. It should perhaps be treated just like the other ornament, as a device to enhance the harmonic or melodic qualities of a particular note. Once again the *bon goût* of the player, and the study of the exactly notated French school, will decide where and how much to apply this most expressive of devices.

Marin Marais, *Le Tombeau pour Mr. de Ste Colombe, Livre II, 1701 p. 111*
with the *coulé du doigt* (slide) in the third bar of line 3 and the two sorts of vibrato in bars 3 and 4 of the last line.

What are the technical lessons of contemporary textual indications?
Composers of the period are almost certainly expecting the player to use the first position and open strings unless there is good reason not to. The inference of this is that the 18th century player would have chosen a difficult bowing rather than a change of position. In this context the frequent changes of position used by the modern player to avoid open strings are out of place. Furthermore, as indicated by De Machy's *tenües* (see above), the player would be seeking to leave bass notes down as much as possible to build up harmonic resonance. Bowings would be as simple as possible and observe the rule of the downbow.

What is the rule of the downbow?
All contemporary authors agree that each bar should start on a downbow, and that immediate adjustment should be made in case of interruption to the normal to and fro of bowing. But closer examination of notated French bowings in the music for bass viol reveals that this rule can be broken if musically necessary. On occasions it might be desirable, for musical effect, to group two bars of a minuet or sarabande together, resulting on an upbow for the second bar.

Did Bach's cellist hold the bow like a viol player?
In general, the cellist in Bach's time held his bow overhand, the viol player with his hand under the bow, but there are notable exceptions. Antonio Vandini (c.1690-1771), who toured with Tartini and also taught for a time at Vivaldi's orphanage, is known to have continued teaching the underhand style on the cello in Padua until at least the 1760s. Charles Burney visiting Padua on 2 August 1770 observed that," *It was remarkable that Antonio [Vandini], and all the other violoncello players here, hold the bow in the old-fashioned way, with the hand under it."*

Charles Burney, *The Present State of Music in France and Italy* (London, 1773), p.142

Meanwhile in Berlin "*M. Graul, a violoncello performer in the king's band, played a concerto; it was well executed, though in the old manner with the hand under the bow.*

*The Present State of Music in Germany, the Netherlands and United Provinces (*London 1773*)*

What was the violist's bow-hold, also used by some cellists?
There are several descriptions by contemporary writers of how to hold the bow, but the clearest and most definitive is that by Danonville.

Le Sieur Danonville *Methode avec laquelle il faut tenir l'archet*
How to hold the bow

L'Archet se prend de la main droite à deux doigts de la hausse: En suite il faut que le second doigt passe entre le crin & le bois pour le tenir plus étendu, & que le premier soit couché le long du bois, le poulce doit appuyer & presser le dedans du bois

The bow is held in the right hand two fingers away from the frog: Then the second finger must be passed between the hair and the stick to hold it on more of its length, and the first finger be laid along the stick, the thumb must press and push on the inside of the stick

Le Sieur Danonville *(L'Art de jouer de la Viole 15.04.1687 Chapitre III p.8)*

What was the normal cellist's bow hold in the baroque era?
Judging by iconographical evidence and descriptions in treatises, it looks as if the eighteenth century cellist held his bow much like his modern counterpart, but usually with the hand some distance away from the frog. Most baroque bows work well if the cellist puts his fourth finger where the modern player puts his first; and some balance better with the hand even further away from the frog. The length of early bows varies widely and the hand needs to adjust to these differences.

What are the grammatical lessons to be learnt from the precisely notated French suites from the generation before Bach?
Bach uses the **t** or **tr** sign in much the same way as later rococo composers, and these two signs (or more likely one sign written sometimes quickly and sometimes with more care) instruct the player to choose the appropriate ornament as dictated by *"le bon goût"*. This can sometimes be a trill but can also range from mordent, percussive trill, high baroque trill with appoggiatura, to *tierce coulée*. These notated trills are quite rare in Anna Magdalena's manuscript and the player was doubtless expected to add ornaments in keeping with the conventions of the time. The later manuscripts and the Paris print add appoggiaturas and passing notes in what would seem like a cavalier manner, but the player of the time would probably have inserted them as a matter of course, or perhaps hardly noticed their addition, since they are an integral part of the music.

C.P.E.Bach (*Versuch über die wahre Art, das Clavier zu spielen, Berlin 1753 p.52*) identifies two basic sorts of ornamentation, which he calls *"unwillkürlich"* and *"willkürlich"*, i.e. the ones the player is expected to do, and those which he is free to do.

Die Manieren lassen sich sehr wohl in zwey Classen abtheilen. Zu der ersten rechne ich diejenigen, welche man theils durch gewisse angenomme Kennzeichen, theils durch wenige kleine Nötgen anzudeuten pflegt; zu der anderen können die übrigen gehören, welche keine Zeichen haben und aus vielen kurtzen Noten bestehen.

There are two sorts of ornaments. Those which are notated either with certain conventional signs or with small notes; and there are those, which do not have a sign but which consist of many short notes.

What is a *tierce coulée* or *coulé de tierce*?

English yields only the clumsiest of translations for this most refined of ornaments, for "flowed third" hardly does justice to an elegant device, which fills out the interval of a third with a short appoggiatura, which, unusually, is played before the beat. The interval itself is nearly always the root and the third of the chord, and both notes are typically *"adoucies"* (softened) with a short appoggiatura before the beat. It probably originates in the seventeenth century French *Air de Cour* and is used to embellish an interval which the French seem to have found too harsh when played or sung without ornament. It usually ends the phrase and is mostly followed by a comma in instrumental music or a breath in song. In French keyboard music this comma is often notated, and one would be at pains to find a piece of French music of the period in which this elegant little device does not occur. Bars 4 and 5 in the second half of the allemande in G are a particularly good example of a sequence of (inconsistently notated) *tierces coulées* followed by unnotated commas. A wind player or singer would breathe after the first beat of both bars.

Bach Allemande in G major from Anna Magdalena's ms. Note the two different notations of the *coulée* in the first and second full bars of the second line: the first notated with its little appoggiatura before the beat and the second almost certainly expected to be similarly executed.

Bars 2 and 4 of the G major sarabande contain stylised or "German" versions of this ornament.

Bach Sarabande in G major from Anna Magdalena's ms.

The *tierce coulée* is perhaps the most cogent example of how familiarity with Bach's French sources can help us to avoid grammatical errors. It can sometimes be hidden in a row of sixteenth notes.

Do I repeat?
Repeats are an integral part of the composition and therefore of the performance. However, the suites now have iconic status, particularly in cello circles, and normal repeat schemes might be abandoned in a recital where the audience is very familiar with the works. The player will make a judgement as to whether the listener needs to hear the material more than once. Some movements, particularly those with a longer second half, have an inkling of sonata form about them. These might well be candidates for suppressing the second repeat.

At some stage the practice of not observing the repeats when going back to the first of a pair of dances must have become widespread. Classical quartets and symphonies are often marked *menuetto da capo senza repliche*. But Quantz (1752) is adamant that "if there are two dots on each side of a double bar, they signify that the piece consists of two parts, and that each part must be played twice" and Türk in his *Neue Klavierschule* of 1798 agrees that "after the Trio of a Minuet we usually find the words Minuetto da Capo, or abbreviated, Min. D.C. This indicates that the Minuet is to be played from the beginning, that is with the prescribed repeats, consequently like the first time, unless *ma senza replica* is explicitly added."

What other unnotated formal or interpretative devices are possible?
Composers of dance music between roughly 1650 and 1750 often notated a *"petite reprise"* or short repeat, usually of the last four bars. This was in addition to the normal second half repeat and could be repeated many times. Marais wrote up to five increasingly ornamented *reprises* in some of his movements and in many instances it is not clear whether the second half **and** *petite reprise* is played, or only the *reprise* itself.

Marin Marais, *Allemande* from Livre V, 1725 p.89, showing multiple *petites reprises*.

Should I be ornamenting or writing *doubles*?

Of all the baroque composers, Bach writes in the most ornamentation as an integral part of the composition. How could we possibly add more to the D major allemande? The status of the suites already make them a special case, and it is a brave player who would try to improve Bach by adding more or composing variations. Indeed most of the music is itself ornamentation or figuration.
We hesitate to ornament Bach in a way that we might not if confronted by a piece of Telemann or Boismortier. In any case the cello is not a convenient instrument for ornamentation, except for the more or less expected addition of appoggiaturas, mordents and trills. Unless tuned in fourths or in thumb position, the cellist does not have all the notes of the scale under the hand so that, unlike the flute, violin or keyboard, he is not immediately able to realise his thoughts with his fingers. One can assume therefore that, in contrast to the bass viol composer/players, who all wrote *variations* or *doubles,* there was no expected tradition of cello ornamentation in this period, except for the obvious and nearly obligatory.

Nicolas Hotman ms Warsaw Ms In.377/No.221 - WTM Sygn.R22/inv.377 f.47 from *"Piesce de Mons. Hauttemant"* showing a *double* or *variation.*

What about pizzicato?

DeMachy mentions pizzicato as one of his four ways of playing the viol.

Je dis que l'on peut jouër de la Violle de trois manières. On peut pareillement la pincer; ce qui pourroit passer pour une quatrième.

I say that there are three ways of playing the viol. Equally one can play pizzicato, which could pass for a fourth.

His three ways are:
1) chordal pieces, best learnt by using tablature
2) accompanying, playing one part while singing the other
3) melodies

Pizzicato and left hand pizzicato (called the "thump" by Tobias Hume in 1605) were known very early on in the history of the viol.

In addition to some pieces involving pizzicato in the normal way like Marin Marais'
Gavotte du goust du Theorbe que l'on peut peut pincer si l'on veut (Livre III 1711)
Gavotte in the theorbo style, which one can play pizzicato if one wants

and the

Rondeau moitié pincé et moitié coup d'archet ou tout coup d'archet si l'on veut (Livre V 1725)
Rondeau half pizzicato and half bowed or all bowed if one prefers

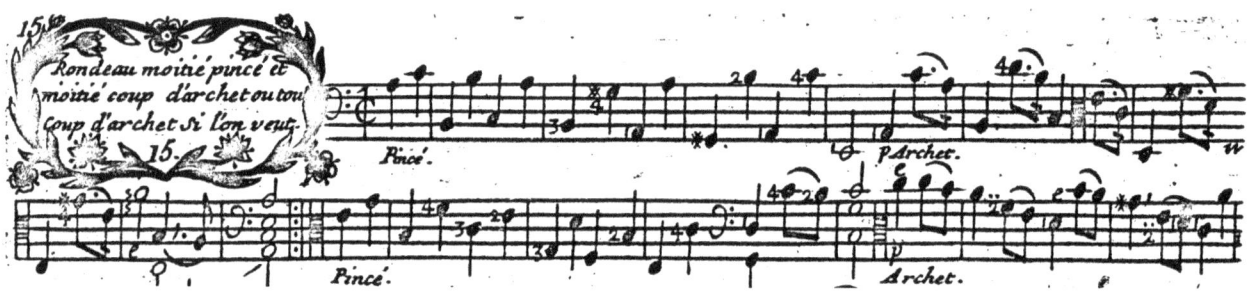

Marin Marais Rondeau Livre V, 1725 p.15

Marin Marais includes, as the very last piece in his fifth and last book of viol pieces of 1725, one called "*Le Tact*", in which left-hand pizzicato alternates with bowed phrases.

Marin Marais Livre V, 1725 p.109

These are certainly among the most exotic of possible contemporary techniques, and using them to vary the repeat of a second menuet, bourrée or gavotte, though justifiable historically, would be a bold decision.

What about adding chords?
Adding chords is a definite feature of permitted ornamentation and some players would perhaps have embellished final notes with an obvious major or minor chord. Adding chords in the body of the pieces is more problematic, since to do so is to choose which harmony is implied. One feature of the writing is its very ambiguity. Mind games are required of the listener, who has to hold one or more parts in his head while another part is dealt with before returning to it. Any harmonic additions will upset this aspect of the concept and will ultimately lessen the challenge and enjoyment of the listener.

In his biography of Bach, Forkel explains how he sees Bach's achievement as a composer of self-contained single lines.

J.N.Forkel *Über Johann Sebastian Bachs Leben, Kunst und Kunstwerke, 1802, p. 61*

Wie weit Bachs Nachdenken und Scharfsinn in der Behandlung der Melodie und Harmonie ging, wie sehr er geneigt war, alle Möglichkeiten in beyden zu erschöpfen, beweiset auch sein Versuch, eine einzige Melodie so einzurichten, daß keine zweyte singbare Stimme dagegen gesetzt werden konnte...

Diesem Versuch haben wir 6 soli für die Violine and 6 andere für das Violoncell* zu verdanken, die ohne alle Begleitung sind, und durchaus keine zweyte singbare Stimme zulassen. Durch besondere Wendungen der Melodie hat er die zur Vollständigkeit der Modulation erforderlichen Töne so in einer einzigen Stimme vereinigt, daß eine zweyte weder nöthig noch möglich ist.

How far Bach's knowledge and discernment went in the treatment of melody and harmony and how great his tendency was to exhaust all the possibilities of both, is shown in his attempt to devise a single melody in such a way that no second part could be added.......

We have this endeavour to thank for the 6 violin and violoncello solos, which are without accompaniment and throughout do not allow for the addition of any other part. By his special turn of phrase he has put together all that is necessary to render an additional part neither necessary nor possible.

* und eine Suite für Viola pomposa. Diese ist eine Kreuzung von Violine und Bratsche, heißt daher mit gleichem Rechte auch Violino pomposo.

* and a suite for viola pomposa. This a cross between a violin and a viola and so can with the same justification be called a violino pomposo.

On the basis of this analysis, any additions to the text, however interesting to devise, would be against at least how Forkel sees the concept of Bach's music.

But Bach himself adds chords and basses in the lute transcription of the fifth suite
One would expect the lute transcription to be more richly laid out than the cello version. But for most of the suite Bach has not added substantially to the material, merely adding some convenient chords and richer cadences. Only in the second gavotte does he write a wholly independent bass line to music which, in the cello version, is resolutely monolineal. Indeed on first hearing, some of the additions are quite surprising, showing how differently each of us will mentally harmonise his line.

What are the musical lessons to be drawn from Bach's immediate and wider environment?
The suites, except in the sarabandes and certain phrases in the allemandes, are not melodic music. A melodic legato approach can therefore be deemed anachronistic, and it seems even possible to infer that the whole mindset of the music is that of exploratory harmonies linked by conventional baroque figuration within the normal dance and abstract structures of the time.

Put another way - where are the great tunes in the suites?

How strictly should I observe the slurs?
Given that our main sources are Anna Magdalena's manuscript and Kellner's copy of a presumed other fair copy, which has not survived, there has to be a certain freedom for the player in interpreting the slurs. Each player must form his own opinion about the validity and accuracy of the markings and ultimately convince an audience of the rightness of these decisions. Nobody wants to listen to a performance in which the performer is not convinced of all details of his playing. It cannot, therefore, be beneficial merely to report the slurs to the listener, if they do not make sense to the performer. But it can be beneficial during the preparation of a performance temporarily to suspend the special status of these works and treat them as if they had been written by Telemann or Graupner, the other contenders for Bach's job in Leipzig. It is not Bach's fault that we have elevated these works to biblical status, and he might well have expected us to change a slur, to add and take away ornaments, and generally to treat these thirty-six pieces like any other works of the period.

Am I right to want to assimilate slurs in one statement of a motif to another where there is no slur (or vice versa) ?
There is a spectrum of opinion between the quasi-religious

1) these markings were written down by Bach's wife in the same house as him; this is as close as I can get to the composer's intentions; I must therefore play them with unswerving dedication,

and the more agnostic

2) although written in the same house as the composer, this is an unreliable manuscript, which looks as if it was copied in haste from a lost fair copy; I will therefore make my own decisions about the bowings.

Most players will end up in a position between these poles, willingly executing the slurs which fall most conveniently under the bow and fingers, and coming to a compromise about those which are less easy to justify, or more difficult to "feel". As in the interpretation of most Western classical music, the performer will have to decide whether the listener is best served by being more reliably reminded of the motif by repeating its articulation, or whether the music is better explained by presenting the motif in a new light, as proposed by a change of key, register or context.

The Preludes: possible models and inspirations?
A chance finding of the preludes with no indication of instrumentation, would elicit the following questions : 1) what instrument are they written for? 2) what are the models which would help us to establish their origin and help us with their interpretation?

Assuming one was unaware of the existence of suites for solo violoncello, one might arrive at the following conjecture:

Suite 1   is clearly written for violoncello due to the extensive use of open strings tuned in fifths and *bariolages* on the same open strings, perhaps in imitation of arpeggiated keyboard preludes.

Suite 2   looks like lute or bass viol music in **the** typical bass viol key in imitation of lute music by Weiss or an unknown German viol player.

Suite 3   is a sort of organ toccata for left hand containing implied fugal sections, improvisatory passages, and chordal paragraphs clearly based around a tuning in fifths and a bottom C string. The "pedal" passages are derived directly from organ music. The first bar contains the building blocks of western music: the scale and triad.

Suite 4   looks like a piece for any plucked instrument (including harp) though the range (bottom C) would point you in the direction of a violoncello in spite of the awkward key and florid style of the 16th note passages. It is the only one called *Preludium*.

Suitte 5   (as Anna Magdalena spells it) is described as "*discordable*" and the tuning or "*accord*" of the four strings is given. The prelude is a hybrid of an Italian toccata with a French overture. The slow dotted section does not return as in the typical Lully overture, but is perhaps suggested by the allemande. It is in cut time in all sources but the Vienna manuscript. The pairing of prelude and fugue was much used by Bach in his keyboard works. The fugue is marked *tres viste* in the lute version and closely resembles the overtures in Silvius Leopold Weiss's sonatas (actually suites) for 13-course lute.

Suite 6   the up and down note-heads point to *bariolage* with open strings and therefore indicate a 5-string violoncello. This movement contains horn-like hunting motifs and might in France have been titled "*Cors de chasse*" or some such.

How rhythmically free can I be in the preludes?
And how should we handle the passages which look as if they should be performed as if improvised?

These are:
G major:
the whole of the second half which is "invented" over an absent but suggested bottom D.
D minor:
the last five measures.
C major:
the rhetorical end with its runs and pauses.
Eb major:
the 16th note link back to the 8th note arpeggios after the central fermata;
the final 16th note flourish.
C minor:
the cadenza like passage in the last five bars of the overture; the rhetorical runs and pauses at the end of the fugue.
D major:
the high 16th note cadenza passage at the beginning of the last paragraph.

Perhaps the safest compromise is to use rubato rather than total improvisatory freedom. It could be that the composer heard these passages in time in his head, and we should probably give him the benefit of the doubt. Put another way, the music is quite satisfactory enough played as on the page and a certain flexibility of rhythm will surely suffice. The performer must make a judgement as to whether he wants to personalise these cadenza-like passages (with the risk of putting too much of his own self in the way of the music); or simply present the music as passed down to us and leave it to speak for itself.

Should I double-dot the C minor overture?
Double-dotting, if it existed at all in the baroque era, was very rare. Experience suggests that a lightness of touch and crisp tempi go a long way to render obsolete all discussion of this supposed rhythmic freedom. But **over**-dotting will occur in any passage where an *inégal* approach is used. In addition, we note that different versions of the same piece (for example the French Overture for keyboard BWV 831) exist with different notations of the typical "overture" figure. In one version a dotted quarter note is followed by three sixteenth notes, while in the other it is followed by three thirty-second notes. Presumably the execution is the same in both versions and not metronomically exact in either. There are similar differences in the violoncello and lute versions of the C minor allemande. It could be claimed that a dotted quarter note followed by three thirty-second notes, though mathematically imprecise, is the perfect notation for the French overture motif.

If we compare the first bar of the C minor allemande in the violoncello and lute versions, a similar freedom of notation can be observed. In the lute version the initial quarter note acquires a dot, and the sixteenth notes become thirty-second notes. If we assume that both versions receive the same execution, then the sixteenth notes in the first and second bars of the cello version become compressed; and those in bars three to five are played as on the page. Thus the piece wavers between overture and normal allemande vocabulary and gives us another example of inexact but ideal notation. It also probably tells us something about the brisk tempo (here cut time) required.

C minor allemande in Anna Magdalena's ms

But how free can I be in the dances?
The dances have passed from danced music to art music and feel very much like pieces which need little or no rubato. However, even while dancing, the dancer can accommodate a certain organic flexibility of rhythm. A case in point would be the *révérences* or inclinations at the end of each half in the allemandes. Surely the *chevalier* would need a little time to doff his plumed hat and execute an elegant flourish with it? But generally the dances need no more than some shaping of the contours with special reference to low passages, which the ear needs more time to understand.

Unlike the preludes no such detective work is necessary for the dances

Allemande
Suite 1   cut C with one upbeat as in keyboard allemandes by Böhm, Weckmann or Buxtehude
Suite 2   C with one upbeat, similar to many French d minor allemandes for bass viol
Suite 3   C with three upbeats as in Bach's 2nd keyboard *partita*
Suite 4   cut C with one upbeat as in keyboard models
Suite 5   cut C with one upbeat and alluding to the first bar from Le Roux's harpsichord suite in F sharp minor from his 1705 collection
Suite 6   C most complex and meditative of the set, and most removed from the original dance

Courante   **French and Italian models**
Suite 1   3/4 Italian running courante
Suite 2   3/4 Italian
Suite 3   3/4 most like Corelli
Suite 4   3/4 Italian with vestiges of Frenchness in the cadential hemiolas, *galant* triplets
Suite 5   3/2 French notation and feel but with little of the complex alternation of 3/2 and 6/4 of the courantes by French composers
Suite 6   3/4 Italian

Five of the six courantes might therefore more properly be called *corrente*. Nevertheless even among the French composers from Hotman (1650?) until Sainte Colombe (1700?) we find Italianate courantes written in 3/4 but typically with hemiolas at the cadences.

Sarabande
Suite 1   Conventional French with equal but different first and second beats
Suite 2   ditto
Suite 3   ditto
Suite 4   more melodic approach with less emphasis on the second beat and some *galant* elements
Suite 5   meditation on the sarabande idea with near total negation of the usual rhythmical hierarchy; a bowed version of French lute music?
Suite 6   return to equal but different first and second beats, notated in 3/2, which French authors call the "*notation blanche*", probably implying a slower tempo.

It is possible that these sarabandes are amongst the slowest in the whole repertoire.

Menuet
Suite 1   Simple pair of "international rococo" minuets alternating major/minor
Suite 2   ditto minor/major

Bourrée
Suite 3   alternating major/minor bourrées, the second marked *piano* in Kellner's copy
Suite 4   two contrasting major bourrées, the second a French character piece

Gavotte
Suite 5   two contrasting major gavottes. The first is marked *en rondeau* in the lute version
Suite 6   ditto, second with typical French *"musette"* (i.e. bagpipe) effects

Gigue   French dotted and and Italian undotted models
Suite 1   no dotted rhythm, hunt motif in 6/8
Suite 2   ditto in 3/8
Suite 3   ditto in 3/8
Suite 4   ostinato elements in 6/8
Suite 5   dotted but notated in 3/4 (also with quotation of the first bar from Le Roux)
Suite 6   6/8 but not dotted

The description of various movements as being either French or Italian needs to be explained for, while the models are ostensibly from those countries, the styles have been softened to suit German tastes and have become what Bach's contemporaries referred to as *Der vermischte Geschmack*, (the mixed style) a fusion of Corelli and Lully's style.

Even in France, composers after Couperin were interested in combining these two basic elements of seventeenth century music.

In Couperin's *Apothéose de Lulli*, a humorous *scena* for two violins and continuo at the end of which "the Peace of Parnassus" is signed between the French and Italians,
Apollon, persuade Lulli, et Corelli, que la réünion des Goüts François et Italien doit faire la perfection de la Musique
Apollo persuades Lully and Corelli that a fusion of the French and Italian styles will produce perfect music.

How are the violin partitas different?
Partita 1 in B minor has the conventional suite with doubles for allemande, courante and sarabande.
Partita 2 in D minor has the conventional suite with a chaconne.
Partita 3 in E major, the only one with a prelude, has only the gigue from the normal suite preceded by a gavotte en rondeau, two menuets and a bourrée - a veritable potpourri of *galanteries*.

What pitch were they played at?
Modern reconstructions of Bach generally use a pitch of a = 415 Hz, a semi-tone below the modern standard of a = 440 Hz. Although this is just a convenience so that organ and harpsichord keyboards can be shifted easily between baroque and modern pitch, it is close enough to Bach's pitch to be considered correct for the period. In fact a pitch standard of between 408 and 411 Hz seems to be the most likely for Saxony in Bach's time.

What tuning did they use?
In the seventeenth century most instruments were tuned in a temperament called "mean-tone". Pure fifths were sacrificed (narrowed) to provide purer major thirds, with the result that only the home keys (up to two or three sharps and flats) are usable. The music of Bach's time requires a much wider spectrum of keys. The Passions and Cantatas have episodes in E major, F sharp minor etc., and the system known as well-tempered (as in the 48 Preludes and Fugues) evolved to cope with this expansion. Equal temperament, in which all semitones are identical (as on the modern piano), was known about as a theoretical possibility, but was not in general use until the 20th century. Bach's player therefore would have used major thirds which are purer (i.e. lower) than on the modern piano and probably tuned his fifths slightly narrow, as he would have had to do when playing with any keyboard instrument.

Every string quartet knows that tuning pure fifths from the C-string of the cello to the E-string of the violin results in an unusably wide major third. The players therefore temper (i.e. narrow) their fifths to achieve a purer third. In essence they divide the interval by which the third is too high equally among the fifths between C and e, exactly like the harpsichord or organ tuner. In the continuo era most cellists 'playing would have been in unison with a well-tempered keyboard instrument. It is likely that he would have stuck to that intonation system when playing alone.

Could Bach dance?
Bach spent from 1700 to 1702 at the *Michaelschule* in Lüneburg, which served to enhance the accomplishments of young aristocrats. Here he would have encountered French music, culture, manners and language, and been taught to dance by Thomas de la Selle, a pupil of the great Jean-Baptiste Lully. It was de la Selle who took Bach to Celle, where an excellent French orchestra would have played dance music, and the keyboard players would have introduced him to Couperin, de Grigny, Dieupart and others. Bach also knew about at least three celebrated French dancing masters in Saxony:
1) Johannes Patsch (1653-1710) studied dancing in Paris and taught his steps at court in Leipzig for close to forty years.
2) The delightfully named Pantaleon Hebenstreit (1667-1750) was dancing master at Weissenfels, Eisenach and Dresden.
3) Jean-Baptiste Volumier (c.1670-1728), whose orchestra Quantz thought the best in Germany, served in Berlin and came to Dresden in 1709.

It is easy to forget the high esteem in which French culture and ideas were held from Louis XIV's apogee until at least the revolution. Bach met Frederick the Great, who reigned in Berlin from 1740 to 1786, in his summer pavilion "*Sanssouci* (free from cares)" in nearby Potsdam in 1747. Here he presented his Musical Offering, composed on a theme submitted, it is diplomatically alleged, by the Emperor himself. Frederick was an overt Francophile, who spoke and wrote to all of his relations in French, invited both Voltaire and the mathematician Maupertius to Berlin, and corresponded at length with D'Alembert and other leading figures of the Enlightenment in Paris. He considered German to be crude and limited, but necessary for communicating with servants and soldiers! French was already well established as the language of prestige, diplomacy and culture, echoes of which we still hear today.

What is a cello in 1715?
The history of the members of the violin family is in no small part contained in the terminology we use to identify them. Readers not conversant with Italian should know that the suffixes -*ino*, -*one* and -*cello* (meaning small, large and small respectively) can be appended to almost any word. (Happily the other much used suffix -*accio* meaning bad, as in *ragazzaccio - bad boy,* has not been enlisted to describe members of the violin family!) If we accept the viola as the starting point, and because early baroque music often has two or three viola parts, the sixteenth century luthier would have made more of them than any other instrument, then it is obvious that the smaller instrument becomes the *violino* and the bass instrument a *violone*. The smaller version of the *violone* then becomes a *violoncello,* with the etymology of the instrument (the little big viola) neatly describing its development.

It looks as if roughly in Bach's time the cello proper had started to settle down to about the size we know today. It was a perfect compromise between being tonally ample enough to provide the bass part to a trio sonata (and soon the string quartet), but small enough for the cellist's hand to be able to share some of the material of the treble instruments. But for string bass instruments generally the seventeenth and eighteenth centuries were a period of flux and experimentation. France preferred the *basse de violon* in Bb, which was not used as a solo instrument and was generally played at a pitch a tone below a = 440 Hz. Its bottom Bb was therefore a modern pitch Ab, only two whole tones above the bottom E string of the modern four-string double bass. The *basse de violon* was also used in Restoration England until Handel arrived with his Italian musicians with their double basses and smaller cellos. The German courts, in thrall as they were to either Italy or Versailles, espoused the instruments which accorded with the prince's cultural tastes - a sort of organological *cuius regio, eius religio* (let the subject take the religion of his master). The Italians had big Bb cellos, which they usually called *violone* (big viola) as the bottom of five part consorts, as well as smaller cellos for chamber and solo music. But Rome and Bologna in particular preferred small five string instruments tuned with one or two fourths at the top. The *ricercares* and sonatas of Domenico Gabrielli in Bologna and the sonatas of Giovanni Lulier (or Giovanni del Violone) in Rome seem particularly disposed to these tunings.

Advances in string making towards the end of the seventeenth century had a significant impact. More mechanised winding machines - possibly imitating those designed to produce the newly popular gold braid for liveries and military uniforms - produced strings which were more tightly and consistently wound. This meant that for a given string length a much lower pitch could be achieved. The larger 17th century cellos or *basses de violon* normally had a back length of about 812mm (32") but in the 1670s and 1680s Andrea Guarnieri and Francesco Ruggieri reduced this to between 738mm and 750mm. Stradivari's *forma buona* of 1710 is 758mm (under 30") with smaller instruments appearing in the 1720s and 30s. Matteo Gofriller in Venice made three sizes of instrument, presumably for the different needs of his clients, and in the 1750s and 60s Gaudagnini made over forty cellos with a back length of just 711mm (28").

It was not until the late 19th century that workshops in France and Germany espoused Stradivari's B model (*forma buona*), establishing it by sheer force of numbers as the industry standard.

Thus
1) the 8-foot G and A *violone*s of seventeenth century Germany could become genuine 16-foot instruments with a D string at the bottom,
2) St.Colombe in France could add a seventh string to the bass viol,
3) the cello - now supported in the orchestra by a manageable 16-foot instrument - could reduce down from Bb *basse de violon* size to more or less that of most of our instruments today.

The cello was now ready for its triple role as orchestral 8-foot, as bass instrument for chamber music, and as occasional soloist for sonatas and concertos.

What does *violone* then mean in Italy and Germany?
As we have discovered, some of the words we take for granted in our standardised world meant different things to different people at different times and places. For example an Italian in the late seventeenth century using the world *violone* might be describing something very like that which we call a cello or bass violin. His counterpart in Germany at the same time might well be referring to a large 8-foot instrument of the viol family with frets, a flat back and five or six strings. Corelli's string basso continuo parts were often published for *violone*. He cannot have meant anything other

than an 8-foot instrument. Indeed it is safe to say that *violone* is the usual word of the time for a cello. The Spaniard Giovanni Lulier, who was working in Rome between about 1680 and 1705 and whose sonatas circulated under the sobriquet *Giovanni del Violone,* was not a double-bassist.

It is likely that throughout most of the seventeenth century and into the eighteenth, the *violone* was played between the knees and the *violoncello (da spalla)* was played on the arm.

What does Anna Magdalena mean by the word violoncello?
Anna Magdalena, in a mixture of Italian and French, entitles her manuscript
"Suites a Violoncello Solo senza Basso composées par Sr. J.S.Bach Maitre de Chapelle."
Suites for Violoncello solo without Bass composed by Mr J.S.Bach, Director of Music

We should perhaps look at a few contemporary sources containing the word violoncello.

J.G.Walther Preacepta der Musicalishen Composition Leipzig 1708
Violoncello ist ein Italiaenisches einer Violadigamba nicht ungleiches Bass-Instrument, wird fast tractiret wie eine Violin, neml. es wird mit der lincken Hande theils gehalten, und die Griffe formiert, theils wird es aber wegen der Schwere an des Rockes Knopff gehänget ....Wird gestimmet wie eine Viola.

The violoncello is an Italian instrument not unlike the viola da gamba, which is played almost like a violin. It is supported partly by the left hand, which stops the notes, and partly by being hung from a coat button because of its weight....... It is tuned like a viola.

This description is amplified in his Musicalishes Lexicon oder Musicalishe Bibliothek of 1732
*Violoncello, die Bassa Viola und Viola di Spala (ital.) sind kleine Baß-Geigen,
in Vergleichung der grössern, mit 4, 5, auch wohl 6 Saiten, worauf man mit leichterer Arbeit als auf den grossen Machinen allerhand geschwinde Sachen, Variationes und Manieren machen kan; insonderheit hat die Viola di Spala, oder Schulter-Viole einen grossen Effect beym Accompagnement, weil sie starck durchschneiden und die Tone rein exprimiren kann. Sie wird mit einem Bande an der Brust befestigt, und gleichsam auf die rechte Schulter gworffen, hat also nichts, das ihren Resonanz im geringsten aufhält oder verhindert....
Die viersaitigten werden wie eine Viola, C. G. d. a. gestimmt und gehen bis ins a'.*

The violoncello, bass viola and viola da spalla (italian) are small bass violins, (in contrast with the larger ones) with 4, 5 and even 6 strings, on which one can play all sorts of fast passages, variations and ornaments with less effort than on the big instruments: the viola da spalla or shoulder-violin has a specially strong effect in accompaniments, because it cuts through well and can express the notes with purity. It is held on the breast with a strap and thrown across the right shoulder, and therefore has nothing which can in anyway prevent or hinder its resonance...... Those with four strings are tuned like a viola, CGDa. and go up to a'.

Johann Gottfried Walther was a close relative of Bach's family via his mother Martha Lämmerhirt. He had various appointments in Weimar between 1707 and his death there in 1748.
Three events in 1708 have significant implications for our discussion of the word *violoncello:*

1) Bach joined Walther in the court orchestra in Weimar. They became such good friends that he was asked to be godfather to Walther's eldest son.

2) Walther dedicated his manuscript treatise *Preacepta der Musicalishen Composition* to the Duke's nephew Johann Ernst. His famous *Musicalisches Lexicon* was published in Leipzig in 1732.

3) Bach's cantata BWV 71 *"Gott ist mein König"* was written for Mühlhausen, some 65k from Weimar, and performed there on February 4th. The cantata has a part for *"violoncello"*, the first so described. The instrument, tuned G-d-a-e, must have been played with violin fingerings, and was probably a *viola da spalla*" hung from a coat button".

In personal and geographical terms therefore we have an extremely close link between Walther's description of the *violoncello,* and the instrument used to play the *violoncello* part of BWV 71. At the same time and in the same place as Walther is describing the *violoncello* as an instrument played almost like a violin but hung from a coat button because of its weight, his friend and colleague Johann Sebastian Bach is writing a part for a cantata performance nearby marked *violoncello*, which is to be played with violin fingerings on an instrument half way between the viola and the normal violoncello and which, most significantly, is written in the first violin part.

It looks very much as if the word *violoncello* can refer to more or less any intermediate instrument small enough to be played on the arm with violin fingering. Mattheson (see below) is clear that it refers to a *Bassa Viola* or *Bassgeige*, leading to the conclusion that, in his opinion at least, we are dealing with an instrument at the pitch of a normal cello, held on the arm.

Johann Mattheson Das Neu-Eröffnete Orchestre Hamburg 1713
Der hervorragende Violoncello, die Bassa Viola und Viola di Spala, sind kleine Bassgeigen/ in Vergleichung der grössern / mit 5 auch wol 6. Sayten/ worauff man mit leichterer Arbeit als auff den grossen Machinen allerhand geschwinde Sachen/ Variatones und Mannieren machen kan. Es wird mit einem Bande an der Brust gefestigt und gleichsam auff die rechte Schulter geworffen.

The excellent Violoncello, the Bassa Viola and Viola di Spala are small bass instruments [in comparison with the bigger ones] with 5 or even 6 strings, on which one can more easily play fast notes and ornaments. It is held against the chest by means of a ribbon and is played on the right shoulder.

"Tuned like a viola". The same strings or the same pitch?
Walther's remark that the violoncello is tuned like a viola is inconclusive, but a strong indication that he means with the same strings as a viola but at the pitch of a cello is contained in Joseph Friedrich Bernhard Caspar Majer's *Museum Musicum*, printed in Schwäbisch Hall in 1732. After plagiarising Mattheson, he shows a scale starting from the bottom C of the cello, rising with violin fingering until the highest note playable in the first position.

He adds that it is

gemeinlich mit 4 starken Saiten bezogen....von vielen aber wird sie zwischen beeden Beinen gehalten.

normally strung with four thick strings.... and many play it between their legs.

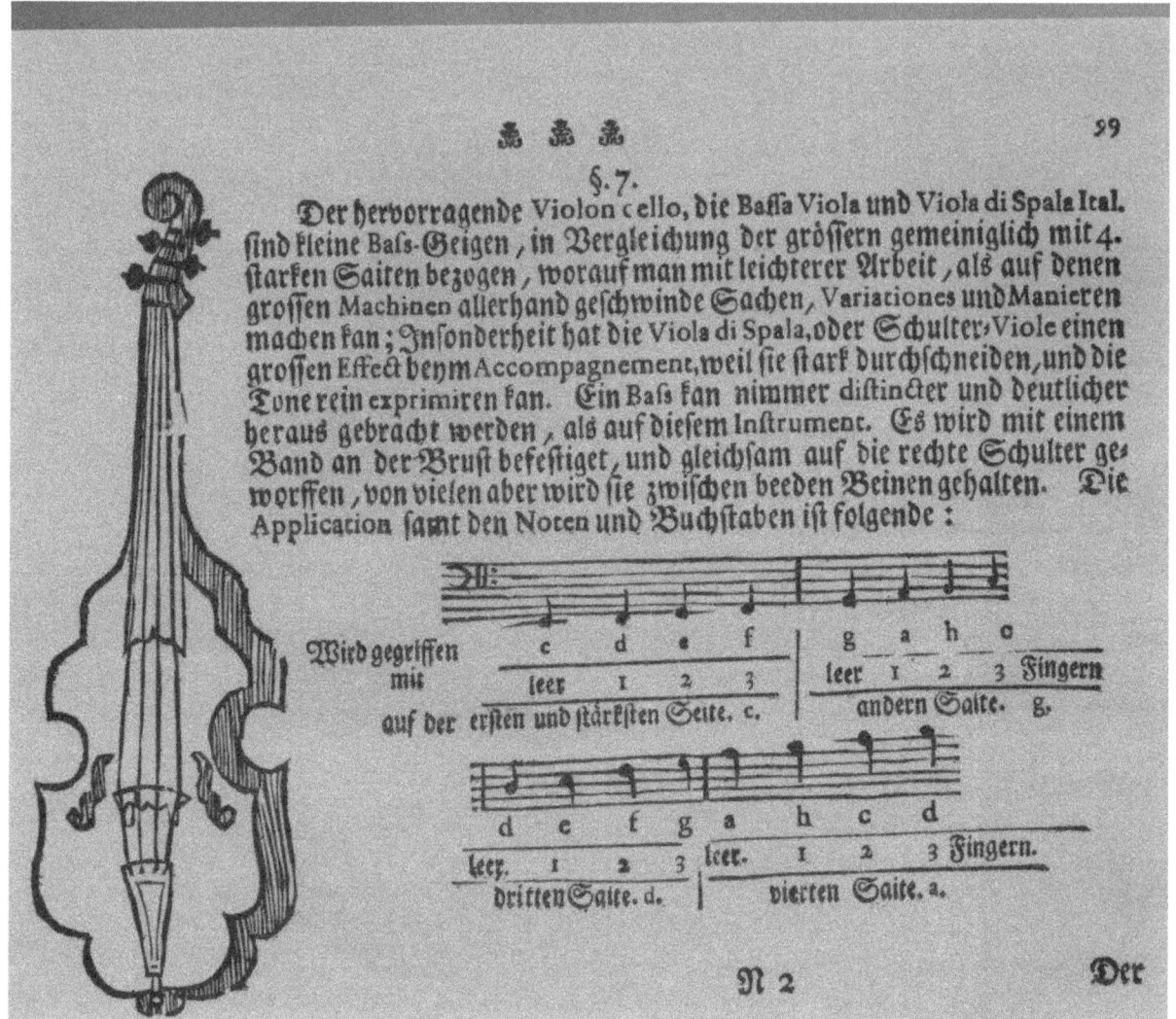

More contemporary descriptions

J.Eisel Musicus autodidaktos Erfurt 1738
Violoncello, Bassa Viola, Viola da Spalla: Wir wollen alle drey in eine Brühe werffen: Denn alles dreyes sind kleine Bass-Geigen.

Violoncello, Bassa Viola, Viola da Spalla: we should throw all three into the same pot, since all three are small bass violins.

Sebastian Brossard Dictionnaire (1703)
Violoncello, C'est proprement nôtre Quinte de Violon ou une petite Basse de Violon à cinq ou six chordes.

Violoncello, This is our Quinte de Violon or a little Basse de Violon with five or six strings.

Vocabulario degli Accademici della Crusca (1729)
Violone: Viola di tuono grave, che si dice anche Basso di Viola, e Violoncello, quando e di minor grandezza.

Violone: low-sounding instrument, which is also called Basso di Viola, and Violoncello when smaller.

Leopold Mozart (1756)
Violoncello: Vor Zeiten hatte es 5. Seyten; itzt geigt man es nur mit vieren.

Violoncello: it used to have 5 strings but is now played with only four.

J. Hawkins (1776)
Violone: it seems that this appellation was formerly given to that instrument which we now call the violoncello

It is striking that Walther and Mattheson, the two writers most closely associated with Bach, are the most clear that the violoncello is played on the arm "almost like a violin" "and hung from a coat button" (Walther) or "held against the chest by means of a ribbon" (Mattheson).

Might cellists have had more than one size instrument?
At the beginning of his 1756 Treatise Leopold Mozart lists the string instruments currently in use:
Die siebente Art heißt das Bassel oder Bassete, welches man, nach dem italiänischen Violoncello, das Violoncell nennet. Vor Zeiten hatte es 5. Seyten; itzt geigt man es nur mit vieren. Es ist das gemeinste Instrument den Baß zu spielen: und obwohl es einige etwas grössere, andere etwas kleinere giebt; so sind sie doch nur der Beseytung nach, folglich nur in der Stärk des Klanges, ein wenig von einenader unterschieden.

The seventh instrument is called the Bassel or Bassete, which, after the Italian, is called the violoncello. It used to have 5 strings but is now played with only four. It is the most common instrument for playing bass parts: and although there are some larger and some smaller ones, the only slight difference is that the stringing is heavier, which gives a stronger tone.

Leopold Mozart Paragraph 2 of Section One of the Introduction (p.3) to his Gründliche Violinschule (*Violin Treatise*), Augsburg 1756

This is endorsed by Johann Joachim Quantz in his 1789 publication *Versuch einer Anweisung die Flöte traversière zu spielen* (Essay on playing the flute*)*

Wer auf dem Violoncell nicht nur accompagniret, sondern auch Solo spielet, thut sehr wohl, wenn er zwey besondere Instrumente hat; eines zu Solo, das andere zum Ripienspielen, bey großen Musiken. Das letztere muß größer, und mit dicken Saiten bezogen seyn, als das erstere. (Chapter XVII, Section IV,

He who not only accompanies, but also plays solos on the violoncello, would do well to have two different instruments; one for solos, the other for playing ripieno in the orchestra. The latter should be larger and have thicker strings than the former

and Leopold Mozart Violinschule Augsburg 1787 Einleitung, erster Abschnitt para. 2,
"Heut zu Tage wird auch Violoncell zwischen die Beine genommen"

These days the violoncello is played between the legs.

The sources point heavily towards a small instrument played on the arm but what does the music tell us?

If we entertain the idea that the suites are for arm cello, we must ask ourselves why the writing is not more like the violin sonatas and partitas with more complicated chords and more extensive fugal treatment. Bach had adequate models in the bass viol pieces of Schenck and others, as well as an extensive violin literature to draw on. The answer could be that the larger instrument simply does not lend itself to fugues and fast abstract treatment.

But we should also wonder how the player should handle the "horizontal" fingerings used by bass violist and lute players (but not by violinists) and probably expected

a) in the second bar of the second half of the G major sarabande, to put the E appoggiatura on the D sharp while holding the bass A, perhaps even for as long as notated

b) in the first bar of the second half of the d minor sarabande to trill on the open string while holding the Eb down

and

c) in the trill in the antepenultimate bar of the C major prelude. Here the choice is between only trilling the B as notated by Anna Magdalena or doing a genuine double trill (common bass viol technique) as marked by Kellner using a horizontal fingering. In either case the parallel sixths of the preceding bar would be extremely awkward using either violin or conventional cello technique.

C major Prelude from in Kellner's ms. Staatsbibliothek Preußischer Kulturbestiz, Berlin, Mus.Ms. Bach P 806

Or was the fingerboard on a *viola da spalla* broad enough for the player to use "horizontal" fingerings just like the violists and lutanists he saw all around him?

Horizontal fingering
is a term borrowed from the viol and refers to a technique used extensively on fretted instruments, whereby a fifth across two strings of the cello (or a fourth on the viol) would be played by adjacent fingers. An example would be playing a C on the A string with the third finger at the same time as playing an F on the D string with the second. Bach and his musicians were surrounded by players using this technique on their lutes and viols, but on a fretless instrument it endangers the intonation and can only be used *in extremis*. Indeed only a very small number of these incidents are found in the suites.

There is evidence that cellists were using violin fingering (that is with a tone between each finger rather than the cellists 'semitone) throughout the baroque era on all but the largest instruments. Between 1738 and 1784 Michel Corrette in Paris published some twenty or so tutors for instruments as varied as the guitar, harp, recorder, *vielle*, and a *"nouvel instrument, La Viole d'Orphée"* next to the more conventional ones. It is therefore with some scepticism that we can view the fingering recommendations in his *"Méthode théorique et pratique pour apprendre en peu de tems le violoncelle dans sa perfection Op. 24 1741"*, (Practical and theoretical method for learning the cello perfectly in a short time), which suggests what amounts to violin fingering. More useful perhaps is the discovery that in the orphanage in Venice where Vivaldi worked, the cello pupils generally received their instruction from the same teachers as the violinists. This suggests that the pupils were using violin fingering on smaller cellos. And this, to a large extent, offers an explanation of the unidiomatic writing encountered in many of Vivaldi's cello pieces.

And what does experience tell us?
Even before investigating the organological sources and confronting the idea that Bach had written the suites for himself to play on a *viola da spalla*, this particular baroque cellist and bass viol player was never quite convinced of their suitability for the mainstream baroque cello. They seemed to stand so clearly outside the organic development of the instrument from consort and continuo bass to the classical (in all senses of the word) cello of the late eighteenth century.

The point at which the same instrument is habitually used for solo playing as in the orchestra cannot be much before Hadyn, Boccherini and Kraft's concerti in the 1770s and 80s.

It seems that up to this point all manner of different solutions to the problem of how to perform as soloist on bass instruments had been put to the test: five-string cello; *violoncello piccolo*; and *viola da spalla*. The suites played on the *da spalla* surely form part of this miscellany.

Violoncello Piccolo or Viola Pomposa
A mid-eighteenth century inventory of the instruments at the Court of Anhalt-Cöthen contained, as item 21: *Ein Violon Cello Piculo mit 5 Seiten von J.C.Hoffman 1731*
a violoncello piccolo with 5 strings by J.C.Hoffman 1731

and as item 22: *Ein Violon Cello Piculo mit 4 Seiten von J.H Ruppert 1724.*
a violoncello piccolo with 4 strings by J.H.Ruppert 1724

Bach asks for various sorts of violoncello piccolo in no fewer than ten of his cantatas, with most appearing in the years 1724 and 1725.

Ulrich Drüner (Bach Jahrbuch 85) identifies three basic sizes of violoncello piccolo:
1) Viola pomposa - broad body, narrow ribs
   Body length 43.2 - 47.2 cm Ribs 5.3 - 7.7cm
2) Saxon Violoncello Piccolo
   Body length 45.5 - 46 cm Ribs 7.7 - 9 cm
3) Larger non-Saxon Violoncello piccolo
   Body length 47.5 - 62.9 cm Ribs 7.6 - 11 cm

The violoncello piccolo seems to have enjoyed considerable popularity, and even cursory research in museums throws up tens of instruments made by such masters as Stainer (Absam 1660?) and Boumeester (Amsterdam 1676), as well as an interesting concentration of instruments by J.C.Hoffmann of Leipzig made in the 1730s and 40s. A Breitkopf catalogue of 1762 lists some forty-five works (all now lost) for violoncello piccolo. The music is nearly always notated in the treble clef (as are the higher passages of the sixth suite in the Paris edition of 1824), and we cannot therefore escape the conjecture that these pieces were played by violinists, especially as the piccolo parts in Bach cantatas were usually written in a violin part. Bach himself left "*zwei violoncelli und ein Basettgen*" (two cellos and a small bass) in his will.

The idea that the sixth suite was written for a "*viola pomposa*" has caught on in many circles. English speakers might tend to connect the word *pomposa* with ceremonies of state (πομπη in Greek means an escort or procession), but the etymology is more likely connected to the french *bombé* (bulging or rounded), meaning simply that a viola has been amplified in some way and is now larger than usual, i.e. pumped up (bomb and pump share the same root). In spite of its delightful name, there is no direct connection between the sixth suite and an instrument, which has received only a handful of mentions in the eighteenth century.
 There is, however, a direct link between the *pomposa* and Bach himself. In a discussion about the appropriate instrument to accompany a violin solo, Johann Nikolaus Forkel finds that a keyboard overwhelms the solo instrument, that a cello leaves too much distance between solo and accompaniment, and that another violin is too similar,

but that

hierinn ein Mittel zu finden, und beyde Extremen zu vermeiden, erfand der ehemalige Kapellmeister in Leipzig, Herr Joh. Sep. Bach, ein Instrument, welche er Viola pomposa nennt. Es wird wie ein Violoncell gestimmet, hat aber in der Höhe eine Saite mehr, ist etwas größer als eine Bratsche, und wird mit einem Bande so befestigt, daß man es vor der Brust und auf dem Arme halten kann.

J. N. Forkel Musikalisches Almanac, Leipzig, 1782 p.34/5

to find a way through these problems, Mr. Joh. Seb. Bach, erstwhile Kapellmeister in Leipzig, invented an instrument, which he calls the viola pomposa. It is tuned like a violoncello, but has one more string at the top, is somewhat larger than a viola, and is held with a strap, so that one can hold it in front of the chest and on the arm.

In Forkel's description, written more than thirty years after Bach's death, his *pomposa* is a large viola. Telemann's 20th *Lection* on page 77 of his *Getreue Musikmeister* (Hamburg 1728) is a sonata with many different performance suggestions, with the upper part designated for "*viola pomposa ò violino*". We can therefore conclude with some certainty that the *pomposa* shares its pitch with the violin and viola, and that the *violoncello piccolo* or *da spalla* shares its pitch with the cello.

As well as a lost manuscript concerto by Johann Gottlieb Graun, there are two duets for flute and *pomposa* by Telemann in his *Getreue Musikmeister*, and a manuscript sonata for flute and "*viola pompofunäbre*". Pompfüneberer, derived from the French "*pompes funèbres,*" (funeral rites), is humoristic German for an undertaker, and still raises a smile in Bavaria and Austria today. The Berlin-based Silesian composer and bass violist Johann Gottlieb Janitsch, who served at the court of Frederick the Great, also left two pieces for *pomposa*. The instrument had five strings and was most likely tuned as Forkel suggests, like a viola but with an e string at the top. Bach's instrument for the sixth suite, and the five-string cello in Charpentier's *Sonate à Huit Parties*, composed in Paris around 1686, were pitched an octave lower.

Is then the violoncello piccolo played on the arm or between the legs?
Once again we have to clear our minds of two centuries of automatically assuming that anything called violoncello is played between the legs. If we take Walther and Mattheson's description of the instrument at face value, is not the violoncello piccolo simply one of those intermediate cello-shaped instruments, secured on a coat button and played on the arm? If so, this could explain why the piccolo parts of BWV 41 and 6 are written in the first and second violin parts respectively. Surely Bach (or another violinist) just put down his violin, picked up his *da spalla*, turned the page, and played the obbligato part assigned to a "violoncello" and notated in the alto and bass clefs.
In BWV 71 the violoncello piccolo part is notated in the alto, tenor and bass clefs in a part marked violoncello. In the same set of parts there is another in the bass clef marked *violone*, suggesting that Bach had both an "arm" and a "leg" cellist for this piece.

How are violoncello piccolo parts notated, and whose part are they written in?
BWV 6   Alto clef in the first violin part
BWV 41   Treble clef in the first viola part
BWV 49   Single page in treble clef
BWV 71   Soprano, alto and bass clef in first violin part
BWV 85   Single page in treble clef
BWV 115   Score notated in alto and bass clef
BWV 175   Single page in tenor and bass clef
BWV 180   Single page in alto clef
BWV 199   Single page in treble clef
BWV 234   Double page continuo part marked "*par Violincello piccolo*" in a later hand

Are there particular passages which look as if they are more suited to violin fingering?
All cello music would be easier to play using violin fingerings and anybody who has heard the suites played on a *viola da spalla* is immediately struck by the relative lack of effort needed by the player. In the diatonic hands of the violinist the suites sound much more like a continuation of or complement to the partitas and sonatas and, especially in the virtuoso sixth suite, one can readily imagine that the same fingers have informed the same brain with a view to performance by the same composer/player.

Passages like the pedal at the end of the C major prelude require no special treatment when played with diatonic fingering, whereas the conventional cellist must either shift incessantly or pick up his thumb, using a technique not in general use until a half a century later.

from the C major Prelude in Anna Magdalena's ms

The effort and struggle of the suites as played by even the very best cellist belong perhaps more properly to the romantic era, when frock-coated elegance and lace cuffs have given way to a more muscular style in which strife and resolution form an integral part of the narrative. We can examine this idea further by comparing the "Sturm und Drang" function of the e minor arpeggios in the development section of Beethoven's A major cello sonata with how elegant and decorous they might have sounded in a piece by a cellist of Boccherini's generation and mindset.

Why are there no bowings and fingerings in the copies? Did Bach practise much?
There no markings or performance aids in any of the copies. This is in striking contrast to the versions we use, which are festooned with bowings, fingerings, dynamics, hairpins, multiple erasures etc. The eighteenth century player needed no such help. He knew the bowing rules and played everything in the first position as a matter of course.

What are the implications of Kellner's description of the instrument to be used for the "Suonaten" as "Le Viola de Basso"

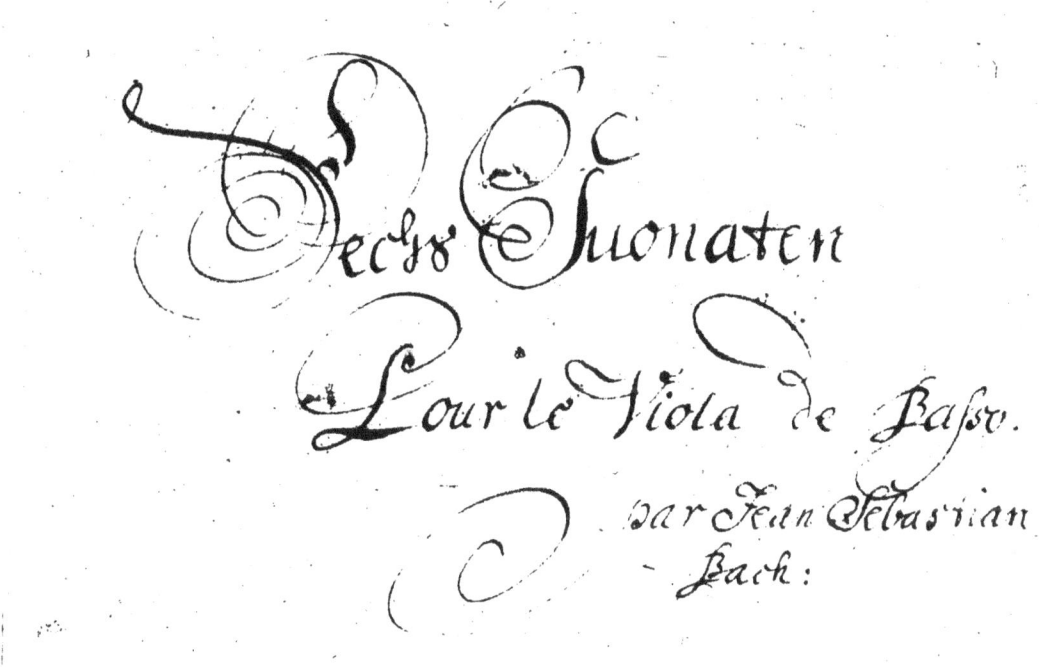

Kellner's title page describes the suites as "*Sechs Suonaten Pour le Viola de Basso par Jean Sebastian Bach*". It would be quite normal in this period to see a bass viol or cello described as Basso di Viola but Kellner's classification is unusual if not unique. Is it possible that he has a viola-style instrument in mind and adds "de Basso" to indicate its pitch? And it is anybody's guess why he veers into (ungrammatical) Italian for "*le Viola de Basso*".

The other sources have respectively: Suiten und Preluden für das Violoncello; and 6 Suite (sic) a Violoncello Solo.

A rare lapse?

The chord in the second bar of the D minor minuet is a rare lapse in Bach's totally idiomatic writing. This is unplayable as a three part chord in which the fingers are held down using the normal playing technique of both the cellist and the violinist.

D minor, menuet premier from Anna Magdalena's ms

What about iconographical evidence?

Various medallions in contemporary or near contemporary prints show musicians playing large violin family instruments hung across their bodies.

How widespread was the use of the *viola da spalla* as bass instrument?

The following example is included, not because of its relevance to the discussion of Bach's instrument, but more as evidence of the widespread use of the word violoncello to mean a *viola da spalla*. The sketch by the violinist Giovanni Pistocchi was found on the inside cover of the first violin part of Giovanni Maria Bononcini's "*Varii fiori del giardino musicale, overo sonate da camera*" printed in Bologna in 1669 (Bibliotheca della Musica di Bologna, I - Bc) and depicts himself and son, Corelli, a theorbo player, and the violinist Antonio Maria Bononcini (1677-1726), the son of the composer, playing some sort of *viola da spalla*. Antonio Maria wrote a lengthy *Laudate Pueri* for soprano, solo violoncello and continuo for San Petronio in Bologna in about 1692. From the double stops, tessitura and general lie of the part (notated in the tenor clef) one can be close to certain that it was not written for an instrument held between the knees. The sonatas of his more famous and widely travelled brother Giovanni Bononcini (1670-1747) were published in London in around 1748 and are described on the title page as being "for two violoncellos". Like most sonatas of the period they are laid out so that they can be played by two cellos with or without keyboard. The bass parts are typical rococo first position continuo parts but the solo parts, which still challenge the modern virtuoso, look as if they might well have been intended for a five string instrument or a *viola da spalla* played with violin fingering.

In his treatise *Il Musico Testore*, (Venice: Bortoli 1706 p.309) Zaccaria Tevo lists the bass instruments which play the bass part in psalms and masses: le Viole da gamba, e da spalla, il Fagotti, e Tromboni, che suonano la parte del Basso,

the violas da gamba and da spalla, bassoons and trombones, which play the bass part

Some decades later Jacob Adlung writes in his *Anleitung zu der musikalsichen Gelarhtheit* (Erfurt 1758) that " *Violoncello* hieß auch *Viola da Spala*"

The *violoncello* also used to be called the *Viola da Spala*

and G.B.Vitali is described as *"suonatore di violone da brazzo"*, player of the cello *da braccio*.

The influence of the lute and its technique

Cellists are not usually familiar with the lute music of Silvius Leopold Weiss (1686-1750), an exact contemporary of Bach, whose music closely resembles the cello suites in the general style and quality, the grouping into sonatas and partitas (i.e. suites), and the use of implied counterpoint and ideal notation. Weiss came from a family of lutanists from central Germany and spent the years 1708-14 in Rome in the service of the future King John Sobieski of Poland. From 1717 onwards he is listed as a member of the Saxon court at Dresden. His first recorded meeting with Bach is in 1739 but his suites were known in Germany from 1706 onwards. Weiss's younger brother Johan Sigismund was not only a lutanist but also viol player, violinist and composer.

The relatively few changes necessary for the transcription of the fifth suite onto the lute (or vice versa) is an indication of how close the styles and idioms of the two instruments are at this period. In Hotman's time, two generations before Bach, players often performed on both instruments. It is also not impossible that the cello suite is a transcription of the lute suite. This would explain its singular nature, its extreme Frenchness, and the tuning of the fourth between the two top strings to accommodate music already conceived with that interval in mind.

In August 1739 Bach's eldest son Wilhelm Friedemann, who was employed in Dresden, visited his father in Leipzig. With him was his friend Weiss and another Dresden lute player called Kropfgans.

The lute transcription of the fifth suite is titled "*Pièces pour la Luth à Monsieur Shouster par J.S.Bach*" (lute pieces for Monsieur Schouster by J.S.Bach). It was probably made at the request of the Leipzig book dealer Jacob Schuster, a friend of Weiss himself, in whose circle we also find lutanists Adam Falkenhagen and Luise Adelgunde Gottsched, woman of letters and wife of the famous music critic Johann Christoph Gottsched.

What is ideal notation?

Ideal notation, quite prevalent in the suites, indicates a musical idea which cannot physically be realised by the player, and which can often be executed in more than one way.
In the first bar of the Eb sarabande the player has at least three options:
1) to leave the lower Eb in order to change bow for the C in the upper part
2) to slur the three upper notes in order to realise the dotted half note in the lower part
3) to tie the first two notes in the bar, which, though not precisely indicated by the notation, has the advantage of playing the lower part for one beat longer and arranges the bowing so that the rule of the down bow can be observed, i.e. with a down bow on the next barline.

It would also be just about feasible, but much less satisfactory, to play the lower Eb three times.

Eb major Sarabande in Anna Magdalena's manuscript

D minor Sarabande in Anna Magdalena's manuscript

In this example only the most double-jointed of players will be able to hold the lower A while executing an elegant conclusion to the trill, here notated but not strictly necessary, as the player would add one as a matter of course, particularly in slow music. (C.P.E.Bach informs us that a trill over a long note always has a conclusion - *hat allezeit einen Nachschlag*). The composer would surely have expected the performer to establish the lower A as the bass, and then devote his attention to the melody.

Should I play by heart?
In our time cellists have so thoroughly interiorised the suites that playing by heart is almost automatic. But given the uncertain function of the music at its inception, it would be difficult to imagine that anyone in Bach's time would have gone to the lengths of committing them to memory. Except for improvisation, playing from music, even for pianists, would have been the norm until well into the third quarter of the nineteenth century. At this time the famous virtuoso Clara Schumann (Robert's widow) complained that the French had started to give their recitals by heart, and that she would henceforth, very unfortunately, be obliged to memorise her pieces!

What are the major innovations?
The suites contain a number of passages with completely new sounds. Effects like the pedal passages at the end of the G major and C major preludes, in the C minor fugue, and those at the end of both halves of the C major gigue would not have been heard on the cello before. To these we must add the many bell effects (common on instruments of the lute family) in the D major prelude, and the chains of sixths in the sarabande of same suite.

What clues do we get from contemporary sources about the character of the keys.
Marc-Antoine Charpentier (1634-1704) describes the characteristics of keys, which he calls
L'Energie des Modes, as follows:
G major: doucement joyeux   gently joyous
D minor: grave et dévot   grave and pious
C major: gai et guerrier   gay and warlike
Eb major: cruel et dur   cruel and harsh
C minor: obscur et triste   dark and sad
D major: joyeux et très guerrier   joyous and very warlike

Jean-Philippe Rameau (1683-1764) in chapter 2 of the second book of his *Traité de l'Harmonie*
of 1722 states that both C major and D major are suitable for:
Chants d'allégresse et de reconnaissance, elation and gratefulness
G major for *chants tendres et gais, ou encore au grand et au magnifique*
  both tender and gay or even grand and magnificent melodies
D minor for *la douceur et à la tendresse,* gentleness and tenderness
C minor for *la tendresse et aux plaintes,* tenderness and laments

But the German writers offer perhaps closer insight into Bach's aesthetic system. The polymath Johann Mattheson (1681-1764) was a friend of Handel, secretary to the English ambassador to Hamburg as well as a fine singer, organist and opera composer. In addition to his twenty or so operas, he wrote copiously about every aspect of musical performance, composition and aesthetics.

In *Das neu-eröffnete Orchestre* (the newly founded orchestra) of 1713 he gives some advice as to the meaning of keys.

G major:
hat viel insinuantes *und redendes in sich; er* brillirt *dabey auch nicht wenig / und ist so wol zu serieusen als munteren Dingen gar geschickt. Athanasius Kircher: [Musurgia universalis, 1650] nennt ihn: "Verliebt und wollüstig." Anderswo auch: " einen ehrlichen Hüter der Mäßigkeit", Corvinus "Er ist den lustigen und verliebten Sachen zugethan."*

has much suggestive and narrative about it; it is not a little brilliant and is suitable for both the serious and the cheerful. Athanasius Kircher *[Musurgia universalis,1650]* calls it " amorous and sensual" and elsewhere "an honest custodian of moderation", Corvinus: "it is suitable for the amusing and amorous".

C major:
hat eine ziemliche rude *und freche Eigenschafft / wird aber zu* rejouissancen, *und wo man sonst der Freude ihren Lauff läst / nicht ungeschickt seyn; dem ungeachtet kan ihn ein* habiler componist *zu gar was* charmantes *umtauffen / und füglich auch in* tendren *Fällen anbringen.*

has a rather crude and cheeky character and will not be unsuitable for *réjouissances* and other music where joy is given free rein; this notwithstanding, a clever composer will be able to modify its use for charming pieces as well, and even in tender music when appropriate.

Eb major:
hat viel patheti*sches an sich; will mit nichts als ernsthafften und dabey* plaintiven *Sachen gerne zu thun haben / ist auch aller Uppigkeit gleichsam spinnefeind.*

has much pathos in it; and should only be associated with serious and plaintive things, it is also the mortal enemy of opulence.

D major:
ist von Natur etwas scharff und eigensinnig; zum Lermen / lustigen / kriegerischen / und auffmunternden Sachen wol am allerbequemsten; doch wird zugleich niemand in Abrede seyn / daß nicht auch dieser harte Tohn / gar artige und frembde Anleitung zu delicaten *Sachen geben könne.*

is somewhat harsh and headstrong by nature; best for noisy, joyous, war-like and rousing music; but at the same time nobody can deny that even this unyielding key can give a pleasing and exotic side to delicate pieces.

However, since both the French writers and Mattheson are probably more attuned to the conventions of opera than to dance suites, we should perhaps also examine the way Bach employs different keys in the St. Matthew and St. John Passions and cantatas.

G major: St.M *Ja nicht auf das Fest* - festive and joyful
D minor: St.J *Von den Strikken meiner Sünden* - anxious and troubled as in the double violin or harpsichord concerto - excited and passionate
C major: St.J *Lasset uns den nicht zerteilen* - headlong movement
Eb major: St.M *Sehet, Jesus hat die Hand* - serene and tortured
           St.J *Betrachte meine Seele* - meditative but tortured
C minor: St.J *Ruhet wohl* - resigned and monumental
           St.J *Erwäge* - crushedly meditative
D major: St.J *Der Held aud Juda siegt mit Macht* - joyous and warlike

Were the suites ever performed at what we might call a concert?
In Bach's time there was as yet no widespread tradition of members of the general public paying to hear art music in purpose-built venues. In Leipzig, chamber music was sometimes performed in *Zimmerman's Kaffeehaus* by the *Collegium Musicum* of the University, founded by Telemann. This series ran for about forty years and ended with the death of Zimmerman himself in 1741. Bach was director of the concerts and transcribed many of his works - particularly harpsichord concertos - for performance there. It is not impossible that a cello suite might also have been performed. Altnikol mentions Bach playing the violin solos on a clavichord adding many notes, presumably as in his transcription of the C major prelude into G major. Buxtehude's *Abendmusik* concerts of chamber music in Lübeck achieved widespread fame in the 1690s and Telemann organised concerts in the Drillhaus in Hamburg from about 1720 onwards. These were unusual enterprises. Similarly Philidor organised the Lent "*Concerts Spirituels*" in Paris from about 1725 onwards, but the emphasis there seems to have been on larger productions than chamber music.

Is there a consistent tempo for dance movements ?
In his *Principes du Clavecin* Michel de Saint-Lambert writes:

C'est ainsi que se battent encore les Menuets à danser, quoy que la Mesure en soit de trois Noires, parce qu'on les joüe fort gayement. Je dis les Menuets à danser; car il y a des Menuets de Clavecin qui ne se joüent pas ordinairement si vîte.

This is how to beat minuets for dancing, which although notated in 3/4 are played very quickly. I am talking about minuets for dancing, since minuets for the harpsichord are not usually played so fast.

Les Principes du Clavecin, Christophe Ballard, Paris 1702 p.47

Nevertheless, in any given place and time there is bound to have been a standard approach to the dances, and it goes more or less without saying that a low instrument might take some tempos more slowly than a flute or violin.

François Couperin exhorts the harpsichordist to play tender music more quickly than on the genuine melody instruments.

What should we make of the common time and cut common time in the allemandes?
In Anna Magdalena's manuscript, the allemandes in G, Eb, and C minor are notated in cut time and those in D minor, and C are in normal common time. It is puzzling that the G, D minor and Eb allemandes, which are quite similar in material, should be differently notated. The difference, if really meant, could refer to the speed of the harmonic movement, which often goes by half bar in the G and Eb pieces but more in quarter notes in the D minor. Of all the allemandes, the C minor is most obviously in two beats in a bar, though notated in simple common time in the two 18th century copies and the Paris print. Similarly one of the early copies has the G major allemande in common time and the Paris edition prints the D minor in cut time. It is also quite possible that composers and copyists of the period were quite uninterested in such details, since everybody at the time knew how an allemande went. Hotman, for example, has extremely similar allemandes with different notation next to each other in his manuscript. If the notation difference has any significance at all, it is perhaps that of the pulse of the harmonic movement.
Bach's C major is a different type altogether and the D major is in a world of its own.

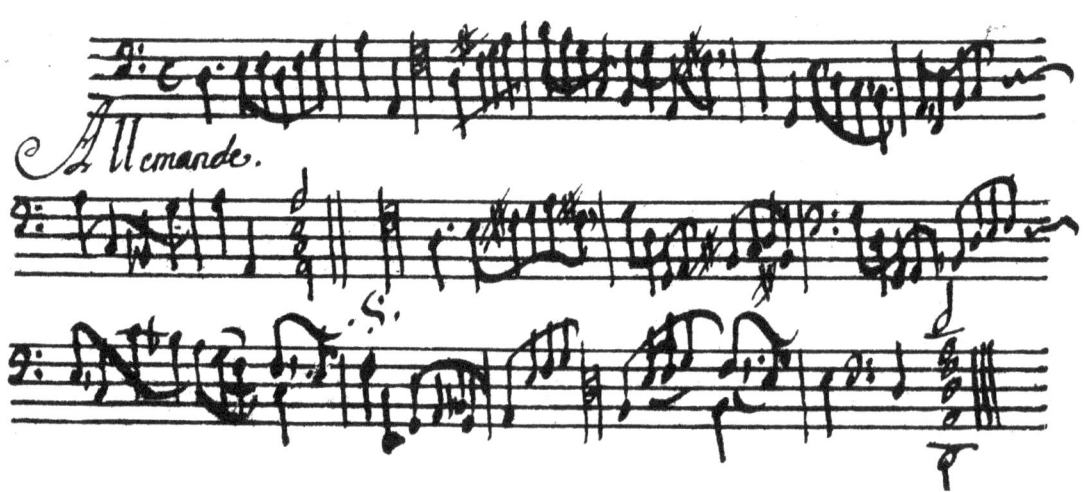

Nicolas Hotman, Warsaw ms f.65 and 69

And the courantes?
All the courantes are notated in 3/4 except the French one in the fifth suite, which is notated in 3/2.

What about dynamics?
Instruments of the period would have produced substantially fewer decibels than their 21st century counterparts. Bach's cellist would have had a dynamic range of pianissimo up to perhaps today's mezzoforte. It is therefore logical that the 18th century cellist would have used other weapons to assist his rhetorical narrative, and dynamics would certainly have been one of these.
The harpsichordist, whose instrument has ostensibly no dynamic range, uses over-legato (i.e. the holding down of notes for longer than indicated by the note values) to augment and reduce volume. The cellist can imitate this technique by leaving down notes, which are useful for building up resonance in harmonic structures.

The Eb prelude: do I play long or short?
A familiar question on courses and in classes! The answer is that every eighth note in each bar has a distinct hierarchical function. The challenge in music of this period is to form groups of notes (in this case, eighth notes) into small dynamic units, which are assembled into longer phrases, in which at all times harmony is the master. These longer phrases then form their own hierarchy within the framework of the whole narrative of the movement. Thus in most of the bars in the Eb prelude, the first and fifth eighth notes are the pillars between which the others are formed into dynamic units. In some cases the second and third result from the first and therefore decrease in importance. In others the second and third lead dynamically to the fifth, with the fourth and eighth serving mostly as upbeat to the pillars. Those eighth notes deemed to be of decreasing importance can be played shorter and shorter, those deemed to be serving as propellants to the next pillar can be played gradually longer and more loudly. The dynamic units can be shaped as much by greater and lesser density of stroke as by crescendo and decrescendo. In deciding on appropriate articulation it is as well to remember the origins of the prelude in the *style luthé* of the French lutanists, who mould the details of their interpretation with resonance and holds rather than differentiation of bow-strokes.

The Eb suite: should I tune the cello up a semitone so that I can play in D major?
Most cellists find the Eb suite problematic and seek a way out. We find ourselves wondering whether Bach conceived the set as three normal suites, and three with different tunings. The mind even wanders as far as the viola part of the Mozart *Sinfonia Concertante* in which the the viola tunes up a semitone to play an Eb piece in what then feels like D major. It is a tempting thought, but one immediately banished by the loss of the bottom C, which is such an integral part of the sound picture. Experienced *da spalla* players will tell you that the Eb suite is a joy to play.

What rhetorical terms of reference are there?
Apart from music, Bach also taught rhetoric and grammar at the Thomasschule in Leipzig, contracted his Latin duties out to another. Help with small scale rhetoric can be found on page 224 of Mattheson's *Vollkommene Kapellmeister* of 1739, where he dissects a minuet into its constituent parts by means of colons, semi-colons, commas, periods and emphases.

Johann Mattheson's rhetorical dissection of a minuet from *Der Vollkommene Capellmeister*, *Hamburg 1739 p.224*

Bach's pupils and indeed any educated musician of the time would have been familiar with this approach. For large scale rhetoric, it can be assumed that advanced students of Latin would have known of Cicero and Quintilian's expansion of the old Aristotelian six-part rhetorical system into the typical *dispositio,* which Mattheson lays out as follows: *exordium* (introduction or exposition), *narratio* (the laying out of the case), *divisio* or *partitio* (the outline of the major points), *confirmatio* (the proof), *confutatio* (the refuting of other arguments), and *peroratio* (summing up). It is tempting to enjoy the coincidence of the suites 'six movements with a system, which is presumably designed for abstract philosophical argument as well as for advocacy in the law courts, and indeed some progress can be made in fitting the one to the other. A case can certainly be made for the prelude as introduction, the allemande as narration, the sarabande as proof, and the gigue as a summing up. It is more difficult to find a *partitio* in the courante, or a *confutatio* in the *galanteries,* unless we accept as polemic the alternating major/minor duality.

Where else can I turn for interpretative help?
The other manuscripts offer some clues to contemporary or near contemporary performance practice.

Kellner has a *piano* in the prelude of the D minor suite, marks the C major prelude *presto*, the second C major bourrée *piano*, has no dynamics in the D major prelude, but marks the allemande *adagio*. Surprisingly, he notates the C minor suite in normal tuning.

Source C has dynamics in the Eb bourrée and marks the D major allemande "*molto adagio*".

The Paris print of 1824 describes the suites as "*Sonates ou Etudes*" and, as well as abundant inaccuracies, has many fingerings, dynamics, daggers, hairpins, interpretation and tempo markings. The chords at the end of the D minor prelude are marked "*arpegio*" and the C major and Eb bourrées have mysteriously metamorphosed into Loure 1 & 2.

What treatises can help with Bach's cello music
a) General performance practice
The few instrumental treatises during Bach's lifetime are for the violin or harpsichord. More general performance practice information can be found in:
Leopold Mozart's *Gründliche Violinschule 1756*
Basic violin tutor

Quantz's *Versuch einer Anweisung die Flöte traversiere zu spielen 1752*
Instructions on playing the traverse flute

C.P.E.Bach's *Versuch über die wahre Art das Clavier zu spielen 1753*
Essay on the true art of playing the clavier

and

Mattheson's extravagantly comprehensive *Volkommene Capellmeister 1739*
The complete music director

The suspicion is that all these treatises more properly deal with the new rococo style emanating from Pergolesi's Italy and taken up avidly in France, Austria and Germany, as well as the specifically north German *"empfindsam"* or "sensitive" style. They are thus less relevant to Bach's music than we would hope. Were it not for Bach we would perhaps hesitate to use the term baroque for music after about 1720. Bach's continued use of the old style, a couple of essays into the new rococo style notwithstanding, is a historical anomaly, and in the context of the times it is understandable that the Leipzig authorities would have preferred the more topical offerings of either Telemann or Graupner for the post of *Kapellmeister* at St. Thomas' in Leipzig.

b) Bowings
The Savoyard violinist Georg Muffat spent the years 1663-9 in Paris learning the French style with Lully and others. After service in Vienna, Prague and Salzburg, he was given leave to visit Rome in the 1680s, where he studied with Pasquini and observed Corelli's music making at close quarters. His *Florilegium Secundum* of 1698, which contains eight long French dance suites, has detailed descriptions (with few surprises) of the bowings to be used in the courante, bourrée, menuet, gavotte and gigue. In addition he outlines the ornaments, which are expected but not necessarily notated.

c) Articulation
Contemporary information about articulation is hard to come by and our best tutors are probably the instruments and bows themselves. The seventeenth century bow was designed essentially to play dance music. By the 1720s it was required to play some lyrical continuo parts and even overtly vocal lines. The stage was set for Bach's cellist to play in a predominantly dance style but with the ability to add real legato when necessary. Likewise the eighteenth century cello is substantially quieter than its modern counterpart but speaks more readily and rewards harmonic playing with longer resonance.

d) Transcriptions

Insights into the implied harmony of certain movements can be gained by studying the lute transcriptions which Bach made for Monsieur Schouster. For example he adds a bass line to the C minor gavottes.

from *Pièces pour La Luth à Monsieur Schouster par J.S.Bach. Bibliothèque Royale, Brussels, II. 4085*

Are there other similar compositions?

Johann Schenck (1660-1712) published a long sonata in A minor for bass viol without accompaniment sometime before 1706 in Amsterdam. All the movements are abstract (including a fugue which closely resembles the style of Bach's fugues for solo violin), except the final italianate gigue, which is unlike any of the gigues for solo cello.

Jean Schenck from *L'Echo Du Danube Op.9, Amsterdam c.1700.* Presto from Sonata VI

Telemann published a four movement sonata da camera (andante - vivace - recitatif/arioso - vivace) for solo bass viol in his *Getreue Musicmeister* of 1728, but there are no elements of the dance suite present.

How should I play chords in this music?

Cet autre signe qui se trouve a côté des accords, marque qu'il fault les séparer en commençant par la basse et continuant jusques à la partie superieure, ce que l'on peut encores appeller harpégant, cela est trés-essentel à certaines piéces, comme celles de la guitarre et du moulinet.

This other sign *(see below)* which you will find next to chords, means that they are to be separated starting with the bass and continuing to the top, which one could call arpeggiated, this is essential in certain pieces, like "*la guitarre*" and "*le moulinet*" (the little windmill).

Marin Marais Pieces de Viole IIIe Livre 1711

The bass viol with its four-, five- and six-part chords (seven string chords are rare) gives food for thought as to the general approach to be considered. Marais 'advice to play the bass in isolation first accords with the general practice of building up resonance, for which of course the bass notes are ideally suited. Taking the typical four string root position cello chord (the first or last of the C major sarabande for example), we can use the bass note for resonance, add the fifth for further richness, and then decide whether to dwell on the third before arriving at the top, perhaps even holding the sixth for some while before isolating the upper melody note. Generally speaking the more slowly we arpeggiate the more resonance we will create.

It goes without saying that the player would be expected to leave all the notes of chords down as much as technically possible. An example of perfect chordal writing is found in the organ toccata-like last paragraph of the C major prelude. Here the player can leave all his fingers down so that the descending scale in the "pedal part" of each chord can be heard to maximum effect. (De Machy or Marais might have indicated this with a tenüe.) This is especially important in the first chord since the dissonant note is in the bass. Two bars later Kellner's chord spacing is clearer than Anna Magdalena's with its doubled third, but more difficult to play. Subsequent chords (even that above the bass D) can be played, with a little ingenuity, as genuine four-part chords.

End of the C major prelude in Anna Magdalena's ms

the same from Kellner with different spacing of the chord above the Eb

What should I do with the chords at the end of the D minor prelude?
One can play the chords as on the page, arpeggiate them as suggested in the Paris print, or add some simple melody to the top part between the chords. In any event the solution should be inconspicuous, since the final cadence is musically the least interesting part of the prelude, and none of these solutions changes what is in essence an extremely simple and typical cadence formula.

There are two much longer arpeggio passages in the D minor chaconne for violin.
In bar 89 he notates an arpeggiation before marking the subsequent bars arpeggio.

In bar 201 (end of the second line) the player is left free to choose his own arpeggiation.

(below) Chaconne in D minor for violin solo, both examples from Bach's fair copy
Staatsbibliothek Preußischer Kulturbestiz, Berlin, Mus.Ms. Bach P 967

Are any of the movements to be played *inégal*
It is well described by Muffat, Couperin and others, that French musicians habitually played rows of eighth notes *inégal* i.e. swung or "dotting them as usual from the first to the second", to use Marais 'phrase. Couperin in his "*L'Art de Toucher le Clavecin*" of 1715 describes this process as follows:

J'ai cru qu'il ne seroit pas inutile de dire un mot sur les mouvemens françois, et la différence qu'ils ont avec ceux des italiens. Il y a selon moy dans notre façon d'ecrire la musique, des deffauts qui se raportent à la manière d'ècrire notre langue. C'est que nous ècrivons différement de ce que nous èxècutons; ce qui fait que les ètrangers joüent notre musique moins bien que nous ne fesons la leur. Au contraire les Italiens ècrivent leur musique dans les vrayes valeurs qu'il l'ont pensèe. Par example. Nous pointons plusieurs croches de suites par degrés-conjoints; Et cependant nous les marquons ègales.

I thought that it would be not unuseful to say some words about the French movements, and the difference between them and the Italian ones. There are in my estimation some shortcomings in our way of notating music, which are similar to the way we write our language. It is that we write differently from how we play, which means that foreigners play our music less well that we play theirs. On the other hand the Italians write their music with the exact note values which they have conceived. For example we dot a row of contiguous eighth notes; but mark them *égales*.

Marais attempts to give some insight into *inégal* playing for allemandes. Regrettably his syntax in the use of the written word does not equal his accomplishments as composer and player!

Marin Marais Avertissement Pièces de Viole IIIe Livre 1701
Les points qui sont au dessus des nottes non liées signifient qu'il faut faire chaque notte égalle, au lieu qu'on les pointe ordinairement de la premiere à la seconde: et lorsqu'ils ne sont point marqués pour ces sortes de mouvemens, on peut encore les faire comme s'ils l'étoient, attendu que le goust de la piece le demande quelquefois naturellement, comme les Allemandes qui n'ont pas besoin de cette observation, et je ne les ay marqués qu'aux endrois qui pouvoient souffrir quelque doute et même dans les basse continües, ces points sont forts en usage chés les Etrangers.

The dots over the non-tied notes mean they are all to be played *égales*, instead of dotting them as usual from the first to the second: and even when they are not marked in these sorts of movements, one can play as if they were, given that the *goût* of the pieces sometimes demands it as a matter of course, like Allemandes, which do not need this observation, and I have only marked them in places where there might be some doubt and even in the bass parts. These dots are very much in use abroad.

In spite of such a comprehensive but incomprehensible introduction, there are only three instances of "cautionary" dots in the viol part and only one in the bass part in the relevant book of pieces. *Charivary* (piece no.58, which means "din" or some such) has dots on all the 8th notes in the first bar, all of which move by step except one. The bass part has no dots when the motive is imitated in bar 2, but the harpsichordist and second bass viol player will have already heard the rhythm of the soloist and be ready to imitate.

Marin Marais Livre III of 1711, p 55 (viol) and p 47 (bass)

But how widespread was *inégalité* in Bach's music?
We can assume that German musicians who knew the French style would have swung their eighth notes in French music in imitation of Lully's style. Indeed the musicians listed at Celle, whom Bach heard as a youth, were categorised as "those who know the French style", and those who did not. Finding places to try out this practice in the suites is more difficult. If we accept that intervals of more than a second, slurred notes even if moving by step, and allemandes (?) are likely to be played *inégal,* then just about the only possible places where we could introduce some *inégalité* would be in a very few short passages in the minuets and bourrées. But in general the slurring precludes such treatment, even in the very French C minor courante. It is far better, therefore, to "swing" pairs of eighth notes, if at all, by releasing the second of them with the bow, giving them a French feel but retaining the essential "Germanness" of the music and its interpretation. Bach was an admirer of François Couperin, famous for his fusion of the French and Italian styles. Is this a style in which the *inégalité* is suppressed as soon as the music contains more italianate elements than French?

What about "swinging" pairs of eighth or quarter notes
It is most unlikely that any Frenchman would have played the D major sarabande in the eighteenth century. If he did, he might have been tempted to swing them, even perhaps as far as the pairs being genuinely *inégales.* A more "German" solution may well be to leave them rhythmically *égales* but play the first of the pair well and the second with less adhesion, i.e. to "swing" them. Contemporary writers talk much of certain notes being "good" and others "bad", usually notes on the main beats versus those on the subordinate ones. And keyboard treatises show how the strong fingers were used for the good notes and the weaker ones for the bad notes. Attempting to play evenly is not prioritised until about the time of Beethoven, as demonstrated by the writings of Czerny for the piano and Duport for the cello.

What do contemporary writers say about the typical characteristics of the dances?

Allemande
Walther (1732): *Die Allemanda welches ernsthaft und gravitätisch gesetzet, auch auf gleicher Art executirt werden muß*

The Allemanda, a serious and weighty composition, which should be interpreted as such.

He explains that it has one or three little notes as upbeat, just as we find in the suites.

Courante
Quantz: *die Courante wird prächtig gespielt*
Courantes are played grandly

Sarabande
Walther: *Die Sarabande ist eine gravitätische und etwas kurze Melodie, welche alleziet zum tanzen den 3/4, zum Spielen aber bisweilen den 3/2 Takt, langsam geschlagen*

The Sarabande is a heavy and rather short melody, which is always danced in 3/4 but is sometime conducted as a 3/2.

Quantz, after caustic remarks about dancers: *es ist bekannt, daß die meisten Tänzer wenig oder nichts von der Music verstehen* it is well known that most dancers know little or nothing about music

writes:
eine Sarabande hat eben dieselbe Bewegung wie Entree, Loure, Courante
a Sarabande has the same tempo as an Entree, Loure, Courante.

He also mentions that dancers are always faster at the evening performance than at the morning rehearsal!

Menuet
The *menuet* was already popular at court in Paris by the 1660s. It could be danced as a solo, *à deux*, in small groups, or as a court set-piece for hierarchical display. It was danced all over Europe and was always considered the most courtly of dances right up until the classical era. Many specialists think it slowed down over time and St. Simon, the somewhat acerbic commentator of life at Versailles, even reports that Louis XIV ordered it to be danced more slowly in later life in view of of his growing corpulence! One popular choreography was for the whole ensemble to dance the first menuet and a chosen soloist, pair or trio (hence the classical minuet and trio) the second.
Both Bach's second menuets for cello can be seen as more intimate than the first.

Since there was such a variety of types and functions for the menuet, it is not surprising that there should be some disagreement about its tempo and spirit. Brossard claims that it is very gay and the movement very fast. Rousseau maintains that the character is one of grave and noble simplicity, moderate rather than quick, and danced more quickly in the theatre than at a ball.

Quantz
Ein Menuet spiele man hebend, und markire die Viertheile mit einem etwas schweren, doch kurzen Bogenstriche.

The Menuet is played in a lifted manner, and the quarter notes are stressed with somewhat heavy but short bowstrokes.

An interesting feature of the menuet is that it is danced hemiolically i.e. the dancer's steps make two 3/4 bars into one 3/2 bar. This could have implications for the bowing, since by analogy with the dance steps, one might want to suspend the rule of the down bow and bow hemiolically i.e. backwards and forwards, resulting in an upbow every two bars.

Of all the dances found in French suites the minuet is the longest surviver, with examples well into the 19th century.

Bourrée
L'Affilard *: fort légèrement* (very lightly), Compan: *à deux tems gais* (in fast duple time), Quantz: *werden lustig, und mit kurtzen und leichten Bogenstriche ausgeführet. Auf jeden Tact kommt ein Pulsschlag*

are played gaily and with short, light bowstrokes. There is a stress on every bar.

Mattheson
ihr eigentliches Abzeichen auf der Zufreidenheit, und einem gefälligen Wesen beruhe, dabey gleichsam etwas unbekümmert oder gelassenes, ein wenig nachläsziges, gemächliches und doch nichts unangenehmes vermacht ist.

Its intrinsic character stems from its contented and amiable spirit, at the same time mixed with something placid or untroubled, not too strict, but unhurried and with nothing unpleasant about it.

Georg Muffat suggests that it is faster than the gavotte.

Gavotte
There seems to be less general agreement about the character and tempo of the gavotte than any other dance. Rousseau gives three different types:
Le mouvement de la Gavotte est ordinairement gracieux, souvent gai, quelquefois aussi tendre & lent

The gavotte is usually elegant, often lively and sometimes even slow and tender.

Walther
welche manchmal hurtig, bisweilen aber auch langsam tractirt wird

which is sometimes lively, sometimes slow in performance.

Marpurg writes that it can be either sad or joyful and many collections contain *a gavotte lente.*

Quantz
Eine Gavotte ist dem Rigaudon fast gleich; wird aber doch im Tempo um etwas gemäßigt

a gavotte is practically the same as a rigaudon but somewhat more moderate in tempo.

Bach's gavottes seem to belong to the *gracieux* category.

Gigue
There are two distinct types of gigue in the suites:

1) the French dotted version as found in the Lully tradition
C minor gigue from Anna Magdalena's ms

2) the straight Italian version as found in the works of Corelli and others.

The Eb gigue from Anna Magdalena's ms

Can I take pairs of dance at different speeds?
In the first, second and fourth Ordre of Couperin's *Les Nations* of 1726 the *Seconde Courante* is marked *un peu plus viste, un peu plus gayement* and *plus gayement* respectively. The marking *un peu plus lent* is not uncommon for a second menuets, bourrées and gavottes. Bach's seem to require more a change of atmosphere than tempo, with (as often in a *da capo* aria) the second part being more intimate and personal than the first.

Does Bach quote any of his own works in the suites?
Especially in later life Bach borrowed ceaselessly from his own works. Religious cantatas became secular, and violin concertos emerged as harpsichord concertos. Apart from transcribing some of the C minor suite for lute (or a G minor lute suite for the cello?), none of the material from the cello suites appears in other works.

There is however a passage in cantata BWV 56 "Ich will den Kreuzstab gerne tragen"
(I will willingly carry the cross) of October 1726 which uses the same sort of figuration as the G major prelude. The cantata narrates the suffering of the disciple of Christ, who tolerates the cross he has to bear, so that he and others can find their way to heaven. The recitative with obligato cello picks up on Matthew 9,1: "and he entered into a boat, and crossed over, and came into his own city". Bach enhances this particularly beautiful text by an unknown poet by depicting the waves and the motion of the boat with gentle cello arpeggios. These cease as soon as the disciple reaches the shore.

Are the suites in any sense a cycle with a religious dimension, like for example the Rosary Sonatas of Biber?
The tradition of solo bass viol suites, which is probably at the origin of the cello suites, has no religious dimension. Indeed it would be difficult to think of any musical form more tied to the chamber and earthly pleasures, or more devoid of any concern for the after-life or spiritual. Tempting as it is to want to explain the Brandenburg concertos in terms of the rhetoric of a Roman orator using one of Quintilian's templates, or (less implausibly) the keyboard toccatas and passion *ariosos* as referring by gematria to individual verses in the bible, it looks as if the six cello suites are just that - six cello suites!

But can dance music be religious music?
Bach used dance music everywhere in his sacred music. The Matthew Passion opens with an enormous pastorale and closes with a sizeable minuet in da capo form. Between these we find three other minuets (*Buß und Reu, Ich will dir mein Herze schenken, Gerne will ich mich bequemen*), a sarabande like movement (*Ach nun ist mein Jesus hin*), a siciliano (*Erbarme dich*), a disembodied sarabande/minuet without basso continuo (*Aus Liebe will mein Heiland sterben*), a polonaise (*Können Tränen*), and a slow gigue (*Mache dich, mein Herze rein*).

Did Bach know the Biber Rosary Sonatas and the Passacaglia for solo violin?
Biber's Rosenkranz or Rosary Sonatas, the last of which is a passacaglia for solo violin which may or may not be part of the sequence, were not published until 1905, and do not seem to have been widely disseminated in manuscript copies. It is therefore anybody's guess whether Bach might have been aware of them. It is much more likely that he knew such works as the programmatic *Biblische Sonaten* of Johann Kuhnau (his predecessor in Leipzig), a series of six keyboard sonatas depicting events from the Old Testament.

Does the fair copy of the violin solos help us decipher Anna Magdalena's manuscript?
The first striking feature of the autograph of the violin solos is how relatively few bowings there are compared with the cello pieces, and how much more accurately they are notated. The E major violin prelude has just a sprinkling of suggestions. The fugues have whole pages without slurs and the *doubles* are very sparsely served with articulation markings. This is partly due to the material, for the lines of eighth notes in the passage work of the fugue episodes are interesting enough in themselves, especially with some varied nuancing of the bow, and do not need extra slurs.
The joyous freedom of these sections will probably be compromised by unnecessary bowings.

Is a slur necessarily a bowing?
Violinists are generally agreed that the bowings in the violin solos "work". i.e. that they are easily playable and have been put there by someone, who perfectly understands the nature and technique of the instrument. This being the case one could very well recommend that they be regarded as integral to their conception, remembering all the while that, in spite of the special status of these works, the eighteenth century accords much more autonomy to the player (who was normally the composer as well) than in later centuries.

Should I be aiming at an "authentic" or "period" performance?
Every cellist, who tackles the suites, takes up a position somewhere between the two *"ad absurdum"* poles.

Position 1) Bach had no electric light so that if I play the suites in the evening, I must of necessity do so by candle light, eschewing my cotton jeans and polyester shirt for wool and leather clothes.

Position 2) As an artist, I have no interest in anything except my own reaction to the notes and will play my trills from the lower note if I feel like it.

Both extreme positions are perfectly tenable on an artistic and intellectual level, but most of us will find ourselves somewhere in the middle of the spectrum in accordance with our education, circumstances, tastes and possibilities.

What does a baroque cello and baroque bow teach us?
The baroque cello is considerably quieter than its modern counterpart, but resonates for significantly longer. The lower bridge and gut strings sacrifice greater decibels for a richer collection of upper partials and a more extensive range of articulation possibilities.

A harmonic approach with much more leaving down of fingers to build up harmony will therefore reap greater rewards than on a modern cello. The baroque bow is designed for dance music and the sound from heel to tip decays much more readily than with a modern Tourte model bow, which is designed for the long legato lines of the nineteenth century. The baroque bow however can, and must be, persuaded to produce a perfect legato, for between the highly articulated elements of the music there are genuinely melodic passages, even if only for very few notes at a time.

Should I play this music on a baroque cello or at least with a baroque bow?
I have performed the suites on a 1720s Perugian cello by Finocchi, which has been converted back to something like its original condition, and a Lorenzo Ventapane made in Naples in around 1805, which is set up for the romantic repertoire with metal strings and a spike. Learning the suites on the baroque instrument with a baroque bow is an education in itself, but there is close to nothing that cannot be realised on conventional modern equipment. I also possess a baroque style five-string cello made by David Rubio in 1985 for the sixth suite, which makes it no more difficult technically than any of the others, and considerably easier than the fourth or fifth suites.

Those not wishing to or not being in a position to change their equipment can get the feeling of a baroque bow by simply holding their normal bow a couple of centimetres away from the frog. However, a baroque bow is not designed to work with metal strings and cannot be expected to do so. It prefers the added friction and resistance of a gut string.

Should I tune down for the fifth suite?
This has to be one of those questions which every individual solves in his own way. Clearly the front-rank virtuoso can only play at his reliable best when playing the instrument he practises daily in its normal tuning. And where does the suite fit in a recital if for twenty minutes the instruments has to be destabilised by tuning down the top string? Cellists are familiar enough with the problems of traveling around with one cello, but with two? So a decision to sacrifice the original tuning (and a few chords) for the reliability demanded of the modern virtuoso is understandable.

But for those deciding to re-programme their hard-won reflexes and learn a new tuning, the rewards are at least threefold:

1) the tuning is the one asked for by the composer
2) the *scordatura* yields wonderful sonorities and new chords
3) it completely removes the problem of playing an E flat or C minor scale smoothly in the passages around the open top g string (as, of course, does performance on a *da spalla*).

But for the conventional cellist, the luxury of avoiding all those stretches or shifts is ample recompense for the initial difficulties of a new tuning.

So Bach presents us with the same dilemma as in the rest of life: do we do one thing really well or many less so?

What about the challenges of sixth suite?
The sixth suite offers a singular challenge, and the virtuoso who performs it on a normal cello must come to terms with the fact that he is attempting to overcome enormous difficulties, which are not originally present. A fifth string and diatonic fingering on a *violoncello da spalla* will immediately remove most of the technical problems: he will not need to simulate the *bariolage* with his missing top e string: he will not need to edit some of the chords; and a muscular *tour de force* on an instrument designed to play bass lines will be replaced by lightness and easeful elegance. Nevertheless if the performer manages to play the suite in a way which does not draw too much attention to the difficulties, he is indeed a virtuoso!

PART 4 MISCELLANEOUS QUESTIONS

****

It cannot be a coincidence that there are six sonatas and partitas for solo violin, and six cello suites. Were they conceived as sets?

The works for solo violin, neatly arranged as they are into three each of sonatas and partitas, look as if they were conceived as a set. The sonatas are *sonatas da chiesa* (church sonatas) with fugues and abstract movements, but without dance movements. The partitas or *sonatas da camera* (chamber sonatas) are actually suites and it is curious that Bach chose to refer to them anachronistically as *partitas,* using vocabulary prevalent in the time of Biber and Pachelbel. They are preserved in an exceptionally handsome autograph manuscript, which has come down to us via Louisa Bach, the daughter of JCF Bach, Johann Sebastian's second youngest surviving son, also known as the Bückeburg Bach from the court near Hannover, where he worked for most of his life. The title page has *"Sei Solo a Violino senza Basso accompagnato, Libro Primo da Joh.Seb.Bach ao (anno) 1720".* The implication of the designation *"libro primo"* could be either that he intended to write another book of violin solos, or that there was a fair copy of the cello suites prepared with the same degree of care and accuracy, which has become separated from the violin pieces. It is surely the ardent wish of every cellist that this copy, if it ever existed, should soon come to light!

Anna Magdalena's copies (Staatsbibliothek zu Berlin Mus.msBach P. 268) of the violin solos and cello suites seem at some stage to have passed into the hands of a certain Georg Heinrich Ludwig Schwanberg (1696-1744), a violinist and organist who was a pupil of Bach in Leipzig in 1727-8.

He wrote the following polyglot potpourri on his wrapper:

Pars 1, Violin Solo, Senza Basso composée par Sr Jean Seb. Bach

Pars 2, Violoncello Solo, Senza Basso composée par Sr J.S. Bach, Maitre de la Chapelle et Directeur de la Musique a Leipsic ecrite par Madame Bachen Son Epouse.

The 48 preludes and fugues, English and French suites, Goldberg variations and Musical Offering are all neatly ordered sets, so it seems likely that Bach, having written six classical suites for violoncello, would have been happy to put down his quill at the end of the last note of the D major suite with the order and symmetry of his compositional world intact.

How unique are Bach's cello suites?
The cellist thinks of the Bach suites as the earliest works in the repertoire of his instrument and unique in its early history. While this is of course true for him and his instrument, they come at the end of a fifty year tradition of suites for solo bass viol.

At first glance it looks as if the cello suites, the Musical Offering, the Well-Tempered Clavier and the Art of Fugue (less so the violin *partitas*) are unique products of Bach's imagination.
But just as the suites are a continuation of the French bass viol suite tradition, the Musical Offering, Well-Tempered Clavier, and Art of Fugue have clear antecedents in Bach's immediate environment.

Johann Theile (1646-1724) lived for a while in Lübeck, where his circle of friends included Buxtehude and Reincken. He later worked in Hamburg and Naumburg. As well as composing a very fine Matthew Passion in 1673, he compiled a *Musikalisches Kunst-Buch,* which (like the Musical Offering) contains a sequence of pieces in varying combinations, utilising a wealth of contrapuntal devices.

The keyboard virtuoso Johann Caspar Ferdinand Fisher (1670-1746) worked in Baden and Rastatt. In 1715 he published his *Ariadne Musica,* containing 20 Preludes and Fugues in all but the most distant keys. The subject of Bach's E major fugue from the second book of the Well-tempered Clavier is taken directly from Fisher's fugue in the same key.

Are they old-fashioned, avant-garde or of their time?
Much of Bach's *oeuvre* can be viewed as not particularly up to date. But the form and style of the suites is similar to other publications and manuscripts of the time. Handel's keyboard suites published in London 1720, and Mattheson's of 1714, also published in London, have broadly the same movements as Bach's.

Who else might have played the suites in the eighteenth century?
Renowned teacher and organist Johann Peter Kellner was born in Gräfenroda, some sixty kilometres from Eisenach, and returned as tutor there from 1722-25, just as Bach was leaving for Leipzig, some two hundred kilometres away. An acquaintance of both Bach and Handel, he made copies of some of the solo violin works and all of the cello suites. Were these copies for teaching purposes or just for his own interest? It is unlikely that they were used in anything resembling a public performance, except possibly in antiquarian circles, and it is difficult to assess the impact of the two other late eighteenth century copies or Janet et Cotelle's edition of c.1824, which describes them as studies. The number of people with any interest in the suites in the eighteenth century is likely to have been very small indeed. Indeed, given the subsequent explosion of interest in these works and the reverence in which they are held, it is not easy to get used to the idea that just one man might have played the suites and all the violoncello piccolo parts himself, and that, apart from a couple of locals, there was no interest whatsoever in our beloved suites.

What about the notation of the sixth suite?
All sources use the alto clef for the higher passages except the Paris print of 1824. This uses the treble clef performed down an octave, and resorts to the wavy line and figure 8 (a notation presumably borrowed from the violin) to denote an octave transposition upwards (i.e. to its real pitch) in the two highest passages in the prelude.

D major prelude from *Six Sonates ou Etudes pour le Violoncelle solo composées par J.Sebastien Bach. Oeuvre Posthume. Chez Janet et Cotelle c. 1824.*

Like so much else in the eighteenth century, there is no consistency in the resolution of the problem of how to notate high passages. Boccherini's engraver uses as many as five clefs in a single movement. Today's cellist can be happy that we have only the bass, tenor and treble clefs to learn. Our instrument is of course a special case because of its exceptional range, and when cellists began to exploit the upper reaches of their fingerboard at the beginning of the nineteenth century, publishers solved the problem of how to notate the high notes in different ways in different places. Since bass viol players in Germany had used the alto clef in print and in manuscript for at least two decades, it is not surprising that Bach chose the alto clef for the higher passages. Schenck in editions between 1690 and 1710, and Höffler in his Nuremberg print of 1695 uses alto and soprano clefs in addition to the bass clef. (Soprano clef is a c-clef on the lowest line of the stave.) English violists like Simpson in the *Division Violist* (1659, 1667 and 1712) were happy to pass through the alto clef into the treble clef. The alto clef would in fact have been a better notation for the cello until the present day, since it produces higher passages without ledger lines than the more usual tenor clef, without sacrificing anything at the lower end. Perhaps publishers were still influenced by church practice, which saw the cello's role as doubling the tenor voice and therefore used the same clef.

Throughout much of the nineteenth century there was a convention that, if you went straight into the treble clef, it was played an octave down, but that if you passed through the tenor clef into treble clef, you played at pitch. To the twenty-first century player the treble clef performed an octave down has no merit whatsoever. He is not used to it and the fact that it is a tone different from the tenor clef can cause some confusion.

Does Bach as a composer develop between suites no.1 and 6?
Playing through all six suites, we do have the feeling that not only does the music become technically more demanding, but that the emotional landscape deepens and the music becomes "bigger", though the D minor and Eb major sarabandes present themselves as exceptions to this. It is worth examining the length of the movements, this being the only objective measure.

	Prelude	Allemande	Courante	Sarabande	Gigue	Menuet I	Menuet II
G major	42	16 + 16	18 + 24	8 + 8	12 + 22	8 + 16	8 + 16
D minor	63	12 + 12	16 + 16	12 + 16	32 + 44	8 + 16	8 + 16
						Bourrée I	Bourée II
C major	88	12 + 12	40 + 44	8 + 16	48 + 60	8 + 20	8 + 16
Eb major	91	16 + 24	26 + 40	12 + 20	10 + 32	12 + 36	4 + 8
						Gavotte I	Gavotte II
C minor	26 + 196	18 + 18	12 + 12	8 + 12	24 + 38	12 + 24	4 + 18
D major	104	8 + 12	28 + 44	8 + 24	28 + 40	8 + 20	4 + 20

As expected, the preludes get longer and more worked out, but among the most surprising discoveries is that, as far as length in bars goes, the D major allemande is the shortest movement in the whole set, except for the G major sarabande and second bourrés and gavottes in the later suites. For the most part the dances are relatively symmetrical, but there is a striking discrepancy between the first and second halves of the first C major bourrée and the second D major gavotte, where a particularly evolved form of *Fortspinnungstechnik* (composition by continual development) is in evidence. Most of the of the movements have a longer second half, and one could make a claim to the effect that these binary movements are slowly edging towards sonata form with its substantially longer second section. Indeed the Eb gigue even has a sort of recapitulation in bar 29, in which we see the composer's desire to present the initial material in the same key. Cellists will recognize this process of "creeping sonata form" in embryonic form in some of Boccherini's sonatas, where the material is developed after the double bar for a mere four bars or so, before reverting to "correct" binary form.

Were players in Bach's time more preoccupied by different bow strokes than we are today?
We can presume that the good eighteenth century cellist had as broad a palette as today's virtuoso. But the very nature of the music, in which gesture, grammar and narrative is paramount, would suggest a more nuanced and rhetorically articulate approach than that of the cellist educated to play the romantic repertoire with its seamless legato and long phrases.

But surely the fine cellist/interpreter of any age will find countless small ways with his bow to inform his audience of his vision of the whole as well as the grammar of the detail?

What about thumb position?
This question has no relevance to the suites, played as they were on an instrument held like a violin, but it may be of interest to cellists in a general sense.

Sometime in the 1740s or 50s cellists began to experiment with the thumb. Violinists were already exploring the upper reaches of their fingerboards and it was only natural that cellists would follow. The first attempts at higher *tessituras* were by means of the fifth string, but cellists soon discovered that, by using their thumb, they could play as high and nimbly as violinists. This technique turned out to be ideal for the sort of rococo ornamentation in which Boccherini and his contemporaries excel.

The thumb gives the cellist one more finger even than the violinist, as demonstrated by Boccherini's unison played with thumb and fourth finger in the second bar.

from Luigi Boccherini's Sonata VI published by Bremner in London c.1770

Among the first (at least in print) to exploit this new technique were:

1) the Neapolitan cellist Salvatore Lanzetti (1710-1780). His Opus I printed in Paris in the 1740s has a limited number of passages in thumb position in the last sonata in the collection

2) M. Canavas l'Aîné (1713-1784), born Canavasso in Turin, who published two collections in Paris in 1767 & 1773

3) the Dutch violinist Pieter Hellendaal (1721-1799), who was active in England from the 1750s onwards and published Eight Solos for cello with basso continuo in Cambridge in about 1780.

At first cellists were not quite sure how to notate this new technique. Both Lanzettei and Canavas use soprano clef as a signal for thumb position but Hellendaal prefers a wavy line under the stave, denoting that the passage is to be played an octave higher and in thumb position.

from Salvatore Lanzetti's Sonata Op.1/12, Amsterdam 1736

This anonymous Parisian print from around 1750 entitled *Concert Italien* shows Domenico Scarlatti, Tartini, (Sam)Martini, Locatelli and Lanzetti playing outdoors with a solitary cat as audience. Lanzetti seems to be playing in *da spalla* mode, though it is quite possible that this is more a satire on how the Italians played than a true depiction of his playing position. But it does seem to show that instruments even as large as the one he his holding were played on the breast. Confusingly, contemporary images also show Lanzetti playing a full-size cello between the knees.

from M. Canavas l'Ainé, *Livre I, Paris 1767*

from Pieter Hellendaal's *Eight Solos for Violoncello, Cambridge c. 1780*

By the time Boccherini's sonatas appeared in the 1770s cellists were evidently supposed to be able to identify thumb position passages without any prompts. While Lanzetti, Canavas and Hellendaal use thumb position somewhat sparingly and, as it were, as excursions from normal cello playing, Boccherini was content to remain there for most of a movement. Indeed the first half of the last movement (the one often omitted in recitals) of the famous A major sonata can, and possibly should be played in just two thumb position throughout: bars 1- 20 (tenor clef) are to be played with the thumb on a/e, bars 21- 36 (alto clef) with the thumb a fifth higher.

from Luigi Boccherini's Sonata VI published by Bremner in London c.1770

Boccherini's thumb defines the key of the music in much the same way as a guitarist uses his *capo tasto*.

An added bonus of this technique is that when the music is repeated a fourth or fifth up or down, the cellist has already learnt the music. He only needs to move his thumb to the relevant position for the new key.

This part of the cello's history can be looked on as the second of three phases:

1) the pre-thumb era of continuo and simple sonatas (many for five-string cello)

2) the era of staying in one thumb position and doing everything possible with the notes available under the hand

3) the post-Duport environment, in which the thumb is just another finger to be called upon at any time in any part of the instrument.

But should we, if we play the suites on the conventional cello, use the thumb in an emergency?
Aside from the sixth suite with its particular set of problems, there are two passages which might profit from an "emergency" use of the thumb.

1) The second bar of the D minor minuet is difficult to explain. The unplayable chord looks like an aberration or copyist's error, but the voice leading and musical logic is perfect and may therefore be an example of "ideal 'notation, rendered possible by the expedient use of a thumb for the Bb.

2) The suspensions in the pedal passage of the C major suite can be executed without recourse to the thumb, but many cellists looking for a fingering in bars 44-51 will have noticed that the thumb can be easily called upon for the seconds on the second sixteenth note of bars 47, 49 and 51 (see example on page 46). This feels right as a temporary expedient even in a pre-thumb environment.

Interpreters of the sixth suite on a four string cello will have to use the thumb repeatedly.
The player will be aware that he is using a technique unknown in the early 1700s.

When did composers start to write virtuoso music for others to play?
From the classical period onwards, we are used to composers writing concertos for others to play. Haydn's concertos for Kraft and Tomasini, and Mozart's for wind are cases in point. François Couperin's *Pièces de Viole* of 1728 may be the first virtuoso pieces not written by the principal performer, followed by the Graun brothers at the court of Frederick the Great in Berlin, who wrote concertos for other members of the court orchestra (and the royal family) between about 1740 and 1780.

The list of virtuosi, who wrote music for themselves, starts in the earliest days of instrumental music and includes all those cited in this book as well as whole schools of violinists like Biber, Corelli, Leclair, Tartini, Locatelli, Guignon etc., and keyboard composers such as Frescobaldi, Chambonnières, Louis and François Couperin, and Duphly. It continues well into the nineteenth century with virtuosi like Paganini, Spohr, Viotti, Vieuxtemps, Wieniawski, Sarasate etc. providing their own material. Cellists will also be familiar with the studies, caprices and concertos of Romberg, Franchomme, Dotzauer, Goltermann, Popper, Grützmacher and Piatti among others, all of whom wrote music for their own use and that of their pupils, as well as to advance their prestige.

The virtuoso who plays only the music of others is a twentieth century phenomenon.

If Bach did not write the suites for himself to play on a *viola da spalla*, who else might have been able to attempt them?
If we are still unconvinced that Bach wrote the suites for himself to play on a *viola da spalla*, we must look for a cellist in rural Saxony with a technique several decades ahead of his nearest rival. We know nothing about the abilities of Christian Bernard Linigke, the court cellist at Cöthen, but if he were a front-rank virtuoso with a technique well ahead of his time, we would expect to find reports of his prowess, music from his pen, or even other pieces by Bach, composed for this exceptional colleague. The chamber music which Bach composed at Cöthen for court use (including the Orchestral Suites and Brandenburg Concertos) demands a certain proficiency from its cellist, but nothing like the elevated demands of the suites. We should perhaps cast our net as far as Berlin and Dresden in search of our elusive virtuoso.

Berlin:
Friedrich I of Prussia (1688-1712) had a court Kapelle of twenty-seven musicians. His successor Friedrich Wilhelm I, *Der Soldatenkönig*, known to English speakers as the Barracks King, was the very model, perhaps even a caricature, of the Prussian soldier, who preferred military matters and Calvinism to the effeminate excesses of art and music. He disbanded his father's Kapelle in 1717. It was very fortunate for some of the musicians that this date coincided with Leopold's desire for a musical establishment in Cöthen, but it does mean that there was no royal musical institution in Berlin between 1717 and 1740, just when we would like to find a candidate for the performance of the suites. In 1740 Frederick the Great acceded to the throne of Prussia and moved his small group of players from Schloß Rheinsberg, some ninety-five kilometres north of Berlin, to Berlin itself. These included the Graun brothers, CPE Bach, and the famous violist Ludwig Christian Hesse. By 1744 he had an orchestra of forty-two players.

The bass-violist Christoph Schaffrath left the service of Frederick the Great in 1744 to work for his sister Maria Amalia. He was among the first in Berlin to show any interest in the cello as solo instrument. There are two surviving quartets by him, probably from the 1750s, which are scored for violin, bass viol, violoncello and continuo. The cello writing is simple, suggests a five string instrument, and closely resembles that of Carl Friedrich Abel.

Dresden:
Friedrich August I *"der Starke"* (1697-1733) and Friedrich August II (1733-1763) dominated all artistic endeavour in Dresden for over half a century. Both rulers understood the political power of the arts, and of opera in particular. Under their music directors Lotti (1717-1719) and Hasse (1731-1756) the court opera establishment, with its complement of Italian singers and instrumentalists, became the most famous in Europe and a worthy successor to Louis XIV's Versailles. In addition to the enormous musical establishment, Dresden retained a troupe of French actors until 1769. Among cellists in the Hofkapelle were the Picinetti brothers and a certain A. de Rossi, but their presence generated no solo cello music. We look in vain for any signs of a school of virtuoso cello playing.

What was the general level of cello playing in and around 1715?
Corelli's concertino cellist plays mostly in the first position but is occasionally asked to play up to the a, an octave above the normal cello's top string. This is still in the first position on a five string instrument with an e string at the top, and it is my assumption that these instruments were freely available in Rome at this time. Even a generation later, the continuo cellist in Handel's orchestra is not asked for more, and the difficult looking solos in Aggripina, Aci, Alexander's Feast, L'Allegro etc. are almost certainly written with a five string instrument or *da spalla* in mind.

Bach's world, except for his rare trips to Berlin and Dresden, was peopled with local musicians, meaning that he seldom came into contact with the illustrious instrumentalists of the day. If the best players of the time in Rome and London were not expected to play more than simple bass lines, how could rural Saxony have thrown up a virtuoso capable of playing the suites? Furthermore, Bach expresses his low opinion of cello playing in Leipzig in his *Kritische Bestandsaufnahme* (critical memorandum) of the 23rd of August 1730, which describes the music establishment he wishes for:

Fernerhin zu gedencken, daß da die 2de Violin meistens, die Viola, Violoncello und Violon aber allezeit (in Ermangelung tüchtigerer subjectorum) mit Schülern habe bestellen müßen……

It is further to be taken into consideration that, since the second violin in most cases, but the viola, violoncello and violone always (due to the lack of capable players) had to be filled by students……..

If the suites are for *viola da spalla*, how did they come to be so readily accepted into the cello repertoire?
Except for a few eccentrics over the ages who were minded to investigate the music of former times, interest in non-contemporary work is an unusual feature of the music world until about the middle of the twentieth century. As the high tide of Victorian optimism finally turned, fewer people were attracted by the ever more abstruse offerings of the composers of that time and music-lovers and musicians had to look back in history to satisfy their curiosity for the new. It is therefore not surprising that there was no tradition of *viola da spalla* playing passed on to future generations by Bach and his circle.

The re-evaluation of the suites therefore took place in an atmosphere in which the cello was decidedly on an upwards trajectory towards equality with the violin. Nobody doubted that the word on Anna Magdalena's title page referred to anything other than the instrument which the Duport brothers, Romberg, Dotzauer etc. had lately well and truly put on the map.

What other "cello" works might have been conceived with the *viola da spalla* in mind?
Vivaldi's cello concertos and sonatas are unaccountably difficult for their time. It is quite possible that the young ladies of the Ospedaletto were exceptionally accomplished players, or that they played small instruments using violin fingerings. The *viola da spalla,* however, represents an even stronger candidate for this repertoire.

In the long list of works whose technical mindset is hard to identify, we find pieces like the concertos by Tartini, CPE Bach, Porpora and Sammartini, sonatas by JCF Bach and very many rococo pieces by the lesser player-composers, whose work has not made the shift to the "modern" fingering system of Boccherini and Haydn. To that list we can add the Bolognese "cellists", Gabrielli and Jacchini, who probably tuned their instruments in a mixture of fifths and fourths. Gabrielli's manuscript is entitled "Sonata à Violoncello solo con il Basso Continuo". The contemporary picture of Bononcini would suggest that he expects a *viola da spalla*.

In this context we can mention Bartolomeo Bismantova's manuscript treatise *Compendio Musicale*, written in 1677 and revised in 1694, which describes a *violoncello da spalla* tuned like the conventional cello, but with the bottom C string raised to D. His fingering chart clearly shows diatonic violin fingering rather than the chromatic system normally used by cellists.

How then did the suites come to light?
Even in the eighteenth century connoisseurs knew about the exceptional music of an obscure *Kantor* from Leipzig. This knowledge was passed on by his famous and widespread sons right up until the "rediscovery" of the Matthew Passion by Felix Mendelssohn in 1829. Since his great aunt Sara Levy had been Wilhelm Friedemann's amanuensis and his grandfather Moses had known Carl Philip in Hamburg, it comes as no surprise that he should have wanted to try out what must have been known in the family to be his greatest work. As conductor of the Berlin Singakademie, Mendelssohn would have had easy access to the many works by Bach in the library there, as well as the means to perform them.

In an age where everything had piano accompaniment it is safe to presume that the works for solo violin and cello, even if they were in circulation, were viewed as archaic and perhaps even un-performable. The thread, it seems, was lost and subsequently taken up by a new breed of cellists. The preface to the 1824 edition by Janet and Cotelle states that Pierre Norblin, the cellist involved in their publication, discovered them after a lengthy search in Germany (*après beaucoup de recherches en Allemagne)*, the implication being that the suites were known about but difficult to obtain.

Conclusion

If the word *"violoncello"* on Anna Magdalena's title page refers to an instrument smaller than our conventional cello, played on the arm using violin fingerings, and if this was the instrument which Bach used to play his own pieces, today's cellist must digest the idea that his beloved suites are not for the instrument which he calls a cello at all, and that he is in effect performing a transcription. This does not mean he should not love and play them any more than he should not play the bass viol sonatas if he chooses, merely that his terms of reference have changed beyond recognition and that his difficulties in the E flat suite, the 6th Brandenburg concerto and much of the concerto repertoire elsewhere are explained. Early music departments and performance practice institutes must therefore face the idea that their baroque cello departments have little or no solo repertoire (beyond a few pieces for five string cello) until the first rococo flowerings of the "real" cello in the 1740s and 50s. This still leaves them the vital task of addressing the craft of basso continuo, the primary function of our instrument until the classical period.

The arguments against the suites being for the conventional cello are indeed compelling, perhaps even conclusive:

1) in the early eighteenth century the composer generally wrote music for himself to play

2) the lexicographers in Bach's immediate circle are clear that the violoncello is held on the arm and played like a violin

3) the instrumental idiom is quite unlike anything written for cello, which Bach calls violone

4) *violoncello* or *violoncello piccolo* parts are habitually written in the violin part (or, in one instance the viola part), suggesting that they are to be played on the arm by the violinist or violist

5) we look in vain for the precocious virtuoso in provincial Saxony, who was at least a generation ahead of his nearest rivals.

Contents

PART I   THE SUITE BEFORE BACH
- p.4 How did the cello suites come about?
  How and when did the classical suite stabilise?
- p.5 How did he arrive at the *Frenchness* of the suites?
  Are there any other French suites for solo bass instrument?
- p.6 Nicolas Hotman
- p.7 M. Dubuisson
  Le Sieur de Machy
- p.8 Marin Marais
  What was the motive for French composers to write all these suites for solo bass viol?
- p.9 What other works for bass viol could have fed Bach's imagination?
  Höffler, Kühnel, Schenck - Four anonymous suites
  Did Bach know the music of the French *Maîtres de viole* ?
- p.10 Ernst Christian Hesse
- p.11 The Suite - A Rough Chronology

PART 2   THE SUITE IN BACH'S TIME
- p.12 Why did Bach write the suites?
- p.13 Title Page of the Well-Tempered Clavier
- p.15 The problems with Anna Magdalena's manuscript
- p.17 Can we make any judgements about Anna Magdalena's script?
- p.18 Which edition should I therefore use?
  Why did Bach include so few "*galanteries*" in the suites?
  Are there other more direct influences?
- p.19 Corelli's pedal passage

PART 3   PERFORMING THE SUITES
- p.20 The technical detail of French bass viol music
- p.21 What is tablature?
- p.22 Should I use vibrato: was it used at that time? were there any rules about when to use it?
- p.23 What are the technical lessons of contemporary textual indications?
  What is the rule of the downbow?
  Did Bach's cellist hold the bow like a viol player?
  What was the violist's bow-hold, also used by some cellists?
- p.24 What was the normal cellist's bow hold in the baroque era?
  What are the grammatical lessons to be learnt from the precisely notated French?
- p.25 What is a *tierce coulée* or *coulé de tierce*?
- p.26 Do I repeat?
  What other un-notated formal or interpretative devices are possible?
- p.27 Should I be ornamenting or writing *doubles*?
  What about pizzicato?

- p.29 What about adding chords?
  But Bach himself adds chords and basses in the lute transcription of the fifth suite
- p.30 What are the musical lessons to be drawn from Bach's immediate and wider environment?
  How strictly should I observe the slurs?
  Am I right to want to assimilate slurs in one statement of a motif to another where there is no slur (or vice versa) ?

p.31 The Preludes: possible models and inspirations?
p.32 How rhythmically free can I be in the preludes?
   Should I double-dot the C minor overture?
p.33 But how free can I be in the dances?
p.34 Unlike the preludes no such detective work is necessary for the dances
p.35 How are the violin partitas different?
   What pitch were they played at?
   What tuning did they use?
p.36 Could Bach dance?
   What is a cello in 1715?
p.37 What does *violone* then mean in Italy and Germany?
p.38 What does Anna Magdalena mean by the word Violoncello?
p.39 "Tuned like a viola." The same strings or the same pitch?
p.40 More contemporary descriptions
p.41 Might cellists have have more than one size instrument?.
p.42 The sources point towards a small instrument played on the arm but what does the music tell us?
p.43 Horizontal fingering
   And what does experience tell us?
p.44 Violoncello Piccolo or Viola Pomposa?
p.45 Is then the violoncello piccolo played on the arm or between the legs?
p.46 How are violoncello piccolo parts notated, and whose part are they written in?
   Are there particular passages which look as if they are more suited to violin fingering?
P.47 Why are there no bowings and fingerings in the copies? Did Bach practise much?
   What are the implications of Kellner's title page?
p.48 A rare lapse?
   What about iconographical evidence?
   How widespread was the use of the *viola da spalla* as bass instrument?
p.49 Viola da spalla
p.50 The influence of the lute and its technique
   What is ideal notation?
p.51 Should I play by heart?
   What are the major innovations?
   What clues do we get from contemporary sources about the character of the keys?
p.53 Were the suites ever performed at what we might call a concert?
   Is there a consistent tempo for dance movements ?
p.54 What should we make of the common time and cut common time in the allemandes?
p.55 And the courantes?
   What about dynamics?
   The Eb prelude: do I play long or short?
   The Eb suite: should I tune the cello up a semitone so that I can play in D major?

p.56 What rhetorical terms of reference are there?
   Where else can I turn for interpretative help?
p.57 What treatises can help with Bach's cello music?
p.58 Are there other similar compositions?
p.59 How should I play chords in this music?
p.60 What should I do with the chords at the end of the D minor prelude?
p.61 Violin arpeggiation
p.62 Are any of the movements to be played in *inégal?*
p.63 But how widespread was *inégalité* in Bach's music?
   What about "swinging" pairs of eighth or quarter notes?

p.64 What do contemporary writers say about the typical characteristics of the dances?
p.66 Can I take pairs of dance at different speeds?
p.67 Does Bach quote any of his own works in the suites?
Are the suites a cycle with religious dimension?
p.68 But can dance music be religious music?
Did Bach know the Biber Rosary Sonatas and the Passacaglia for solo violin?
Does the fair copy of the violin solos help us decipher Anna Magdalena's manuscript?
Is a slur necessarily a bowing?
Should I be aiming at an "authentic" or "period" performance?
p.69 What does a baroque cello and baroque bow teach us?
Should I play this music on a baroque cello or at least with a baroque bow?
Should I tune down for the fifth suite?
p.70 What about the challenges of sixth suite?

PART 4   MISCELLANEOUS QUESTIONS
p.71 There are six sonatas and partitas for solo violin and six cello suites.
Were they conceived as sets?
p.72 How unique are Bach's cello suites?
Are they old-fashioned, avant-garde or of their time?
Who else might have played the suites in the eighteenth century?
p.73 What about the notation of the sixth suite?
p.74 Does Bach as a composer develop between suites no.1 and 6?
Were players in Bach's time more preoccupied by different bow strokes than we are today?
p.75 What about thumb position?
p.76 Lanzetti
p.77 Canavas
p.78 Hellendaal
p.79 Boccherini
p.80 But should we use the thumb in an emergency?
When did composers start to write virtuoso music for others to play?
p.81 If Bach did not write the suites for himself, who else might have been able to attempt them?
Berlin and Dresden
p.82 What was the general level of cello playing in and around 1715?
If the suites are for *da spalla*, how did they come to be so readily accepted into the cello repertoire?
p.83 What other "cello" works might have been conceived with the *viola da spalla* in mind?
How then did the suites come to light?
p.84 Conclusion

Alphabetical index

Abel p.14
Anna Magdalena manuscript p.15,17
Arpeggios p.60

Bach, CPE p.14, 24
Biber p.12, 21, 67
Boccherini p.75
Bow hold p.23, 24
Burney p.23

Canavas p.75, 77
Cello history p.36
Chords p.29, 59
Corelli p.19, 37, 48, 57, 66

Dance characteristics p.64
Danonville p.23
de Machy prelude p.4, 7, 20, ornaments 21, tablature 21, 22, pizzicato 27
Doubles p.27
Double-dotting p.32
Downbow rule p.23
Dubuisson p.7

Forkel letter p.14

Galanteries p.18

Hellendaal p.78
Hesse, Ernst Christian p.10
Horizontal fingering p.43
Hotman, Nicolas p.6, 27
Hume, Tobias p.28

Ideal notation p.50
Inégalité p.62

Kellner p.15, 43, 47, 56, 59, 60, 72
Key characteristics p.51

Lanzetti p.75, 76
Le Roux p.18
Linigke p.14
Lute p.15, 31, 33, 50, 58
Lyra viol p.21
Marais, Marin p.7, 8, 10, 11, 21, 22, 26, 28, 59, inégalité 62, 63
Mattheson p.10, 39, 41, 45, 52, 53, 56, 57, 65, 72

Petite reprise p.26

Pitch p.35
Pizzicato p.28
Preludes etc. p.31, 32,
    Eb p.55
      D minor end p.60

Repeats p.26
Rousseau, Jean p.6

Sainte-Colombe p.6, 7
Schenck, Johann p.9, 58
Suites, chronology p.11
    edition p.18
    four anonymous p.9
    french for solo bass instrument p. 5
    fifth Bach, tuning down p.69
    Paris edition p.15
    sixth Bach, notation p.73
    stabilisation of form p.4
    why written p.12
Shouster p.15
Simpson, Christopher p.20
Slurs p.30 assimilation of, p.30

Tablature p.21, 22
Tempo p.53
Thumb position p.75
Tierce coulée p.25
Tuning p.35

Vandini p.23
Vibrato left hand p.20, 22
Viola pomposa p.44, 45
    da spalla p.43, 44, 45, 46, 48, 81, 82
Violin partitas p.16, 17
Violoncello description p.36
        piccolo p. 44
Violone p.37

Walther p.38, 64

The Sources

A)
Anna Magdalena's manuscript
Staatsbibliothek zu Berlin - Preußischer Kulturbesitz, Mus.ms.Bach P269

B)
Johann Peter Kellner's manuscript c. 1726
Staatsbibliothek zu Berlin - Preußischer Kulturbesitz, Mus.ms.Bach P 804

C)
Anonymous manuscript
Staatsbibliothek zu Berlin - Preußischer Kulturbesitz, Mus.ms.Bach P 289
probably belonged at some stage to Johann Christoph Westphal
and was prepared by two different copyists

D)
Anonymous manuscript
Österreichische Nationalbibliothek Wien, Mus. Hs 5007
had found its way to a Viennese saleroom by 1799
of mid- or north-German provenance

E)
Six Sonates ou Etudes pour le Violoncelle Solo composées par J.Sebastien Bach. Oeuvre Posthume.
Published in Paris c.1824 by Janet et Cotelle.
Prepared by Louis Norblin (1781-1854), cello professor at the Conservatoire.

F)
Pièces pour La Luth à Monsieur Schouster par J.S.Bach.
Bibliothèque Royale, Brussels, II. 4085

Front cover design by Ingrid Seifert

www.ingramcontent.com/pod-product-compliance
Lightning Source LLC
Chambersburg PA
CBHW042020090526
44590CB00030B/4347